IN PLAIN VIEW

LIFE. LOVE. LESSONS LEARNED.

Also By
Leonard Woolsey

In Plain View: A Journey of Discovering Life Through Others

IN PLAIN VIEW

LIFE. LOVE. LESSONS LEARNED.

By Leonard Woolsey

broken moon media
www.brokenmoonmedia.com

First published by Broken Moon Media 10/11

ISBN: 978-0615448527

Library of Congress Control Number: 2011936958

Printed in the United States of America

Edited by Rebecca Rowland Leftwich

Broken Moon Media and its logo are trademarks of Broken Moon Media.

For more information, please contact: Broken Moon Media, 104 Amhurst Way, Carrollton, GA 30117

Dedication

To Maryrine, Alec and Allysondra:

Thank you for your love, support and guidance.
With you I feel as if I am on the most exciting and
fulfilling journey a man can travel.
I love each you with all my heart.

IN PLAIN VIEW

LIFE. LOVE. LESSONS LEARNED.

Contents

Author's Note

Thank you for taking time to read this somewhat eclectic collection of short stories and columns from my daily life. Written and published over a period of several years, these pieces are both very personal and special to me. I'm excited we can share them together.

I don't believe I see the world any differently from you or anyone else for that matter. Actually, one of the most rewarding aspects of publishing these stories is the feedback from readers who've experienced the very same emotions and feelings I'm discovering along this journey.

Life, I'm realizing, is a collection of moments in time. Our personal decision on how to embrace them, however, makes all the difference in the world.

May God bless you and your loved ones. ●

Leonard Woolsey

1 Dragons and Bookmarks

Recently I've begun to wonder when I'll read aloud my last book.

That thought crossed my mind the other night while I was sitting on the edge of my daughter's bed, closing a book about a kind-hearted dragon who likes to write poetry.

At 9 years old, my daughter can easily read any book in front of her. We both know she doesn't need me to sit with her at night and read stories. Fortunately, some habits are more difficult than others to break.

Very few words are harder for me to resist than, "Dad, can you read to me tonight?"

As parents, we sometimes kid ourselves into thinking things will always be the way they are. That is, until they're not.

And so it goes these days for me as our children continue to grow.

My 13-year-old son and I still share books, but on a slightly different level. Instead of sitting on the edge of his bed, we discuss books on the way to school each morning.

"Guess what happened last night in '1984'?" he says. "The main character's job is to rewrite history to agree with what the Ministry of Truth said happened."

"Really?" I say.

"Yes, he went back and fixed the history. Can you believe that?"

For the next eight minutes we will discuss how the themes in George Orwell's book can be found in the world around us. My son is surprised at the book's relevance today.

Our discussion seems far removed from dragons that breathe poetry instead of fire, but it's not, really. Books always have been an important part of our family. We started early, reading together. The children followed the rhythm of pictures and words, eventually unlocking the mystery of each letter. There came a day when I paraphrased and they protested -- "No, that's not what it says!" -- and I was done. The spell was broken.

I remember when chapter books slowly began to replace picture books in my son's room. At the time, I acknowledged the milestone for him, not recognizing one for me at the same time. Eventually, I'd find him reading before bed, not waiting for -- or needing -- me to help.

So as I close the colorful, hardcover picture book about the friendly, poetry-breathing dragon, I can't help wondering if my daughter and I also are on our final mile of reading books together at night.

Kissing her goodnight, I place the book down beside her bed. As I turn out the lights I see the dragon book leaning against her bookshelf, surrounded by chapter books and a handful of magazines featuring clothes and music. Books she reads without me are now populating her room at every turn.

I hope she'll continue to believe in dragons for a little longer. At least, just for the two of us. ●

2 Mothers Plant Seeds to Life

"It's the thought that counts."

Quick, whom do you picture when you think of that phrase? Probably your mother or grandmother, right?

Well, today is a good day to reflect, think and do something about those words.

Mother's Day is not just another reason for the greeting card industry to roll out a new line of products for us to pick through, searching for just the right sentiment. Rather, it is a wonderful opportunity to reach out and make a difference in the day of an influential person in our world. Cards, flowers and gifts are part of how we celebrate this special day, yes, but most of us have more invested in the celebration of this particular holiday than anything that can be purchased with our credit cards. Much more.

Another old saying, "We are the sum of our parts," may make you think about who you are today. Somewhere inside — probably not too deep — you'll find tiny deposits of wisdom and guidance, values placed there by your mother.

Part of a mother's responsibility is to be a "planter of seeds," knowing they will not sprout until days mother and child are separated by time and space. One day, Mother knows, her child will be well beyond reach of the apron string, and he will need to make life-impacting decisions. It is then those seeds will be awakened, to break through from the ground and provide fruit. That will be a Mother's greatest and most difficult undertaking.

Each and every moment is a lesson for children. Long, scheduled lectures are just not part of the program, nor are they effective. Lessons tend to be taught one situation at a time, and they are generally unplanned.

It sounds strange, but today, as the father of two young children, I find myself continuously flipping through the pages of mental notes left behind by my mother long ago — only the notes are now my instincts. I am the fruit of her plantings to a great extent, striving to make choices consistent with the seeds she planted when I was a child. And though my mother is not here today to approve my choices, I always work hard to make sure my actions would make her proud.

And so my life today is a testament to the power of seeds planted by a mother.

I invite you to think about the seeds planted in you long ago and how they have worked to serve you well. Some are planted with love, others with conflict, but all are planted for our benefit nonetheless. This Mother's Day, take a moment to search yourself for one of those seeds. Reflect on how it has impacted your life and say thank you. Pick up the phone, drive across town -- just make sure you do it. Remember, long after the flowers wilt and the greeting cards come down from the mantelpiece, it's still the thought that counts.

I have that one on pretty good authority. ●

3 The Lost Art of the Nap

Recently I have rediscovered the long lost art of the nap.

The nap may be much maligned by non-practitioners for the apparent lack of effort required, but I believe it is time for society to recognize the amazing benefits this effective exercise in restraint -- one known to enlightened cultures of the world for many generations -- can provide.

I'm not talking about making up for a late night on the town or adjusting our internal clocks after a cross-country flight. The art of the nap is about a well-planned and executed action designed to reward and refresh the body, mind and spirit.

Regardless of common predispositions and misconceptions, the art of the nap requires a committed and sophisticated regimen for maximum benefit. The weak of spirit need not apply.

Non-practitioners should understand several principles. The art of the nap has nothing to do with sleeping away long stretches of daylight. A nap, much like an exercise designed specifically to target and work the biceps, creates a change in the body's regular routine. A nap, therefore, must be viewed as a health strategy, not a casual attempt to get out of mowing the lawn. My training routine -- completely unsupported by science -- is based on a personal commitment to making regular time for my exercise in relaxation for maximum benefit to my body.

Time: You must learn to listen to your body. An

integral part of any fitness routine, listening to your body plays a key role in the art of the nap. First ask yourself these questions: Why am I tired? If I nap, am I just "time-shifting"? (Note: Time-shifting commonly is defined as the process of attempting to re-cover sleep lost in the past 24 hours.) Proper practice of the art of the nap involves capturing time before it is expended, extending your energy level later that day. A proactive management tool, if you will.

Commitment: The proper implementation of this program requires careful planning – and sticking with the plan -- to reach your objective. For example: "No, I don't want to go shopping. I have my nap to take at 4 p.m." Such discipline is difficult, but well worth it. Remember, the most common excuse for not exer-cising is "I don't have time." Successful people make the time for things that are important.

Place: Much as with exercise equipment, a designated place for your nap helps makes you much more inclined to stick with the program. Equipment need not be fancy. A simple sofa, a bed and a recliner have, over time, proved to be nap-worthy. Unlike many home health programs, expensive, cumbersome equipment is not required for successful napping.

Duration: A nap, if properly implemented, is not a mara-thon. Much like wind sprints, a nap should be performed in a manner that jolts the body out of its regular routine, optimizing the exercise. Medical opinions vary on other factors, but it is commonly agreed that naps which interrupt the deep sleep cycle can be counterproductive in refreshing the body. Naps should be kept inside a window of no less than 10 but no more than 60 minutes. You may need to experiment to discover your personal zone. When in doubt, listen to your body.

Final advice: Take it slowly at first. Let your body adjust to the new regimen. Allow your body to release tension by taking deep, cleansing breaths before you settle deep into your nap.

And remember, art is something we all do differently. Experi-ment. Be open to suggestions. Explore. And celebrate the art of the nap. ●

4 Growing Up Never Stops

"You just don't understand. Growing up is not easy."

Regardless of what our children believe, this is not a phrase exclusively reserved for the teenage years.

I spoke those very words in teenage frustration as I began changing on both the inside and the outside. I realize that my children eventually will experience the same frustration, maybe even use the same phrase. Problem is, I didn't expect the sentiment to accompany me for my entire life.

As an adult, it's not about dating, cars or the meaning of life. Those questions, to my surprise, seem to have resolved themselves. No, growing up at my age is far more complicated.

Life is, in the end, about life. And death. Once on their feet, teenagers stumble into adulthood. Relationships blossom, careers solidify and children arrive. We experience our first taste of the highs and lows life brings, each event becoming more precious and gut-wrenching as we mature.

In case you haven't noticed, there is no rest area on the road of life.

I guess the first time this came home to me was several years ago when my mother-in-law became ill. As children, we believe parents are there forever, the pillars of your life, people you can always turn to. They represent unconditional love in its purest form. But with my mother-in-law's illness came a new reality. As the adult realization was taking hold of me, my wife was moving across the country into a chair beside her mother, where she stayed until the very end.

Months passed. No questions asked, no answers required. When the full picture of life suddenly comes into razor-sharp focus, you naturally adjust to the scars.

Just when we adults think we have life figured out, the playing field changes before our very eyes – just like when we were teenagers. Only now, our roles also change. We switch places with our parents, replacing them in lifelong, sacred positions.

As the acting adults, we become responsible for the same people who held out their fingers for us to grasp as we struggled to take our first steps on rubbery infant legs. Our new responsibilities force us to cross invisible lines, to make crucial decisions about private details we aren't comfortable even discussing.

But this chapter is not about death, believe it or not. It is about life and how we live inside of it.

Middle life has us growing up in a new and different way. On one hand, we are raising our children to one day independently manage not only their affairs, but also ours. On the other hand, we are being forced to accept that the solid supports in our lives — particularly our parents — will not always be there. Decisions must be made and plans put into motion, but they all fly in the face of our long-standing belief that our parents' part of the equation will forever be constant.

This stage brings much uncertainly, but one thing I'm beginning to realize is that I'll never be done growing up. ●

5 Funerals Remind Us to Live

There are some things in life you never want to get good at. Speaking at funerals, for instance is one. Unfortunately, this is becoming an increasingly regular occurrence as the years pass.

With the passing of my last living uncle, I have become painfully aware of life's clock, of its steady, all-consuming march and its utter disregard for my opinion on the matter.

In my youth, funerals seemed relatively few and far between. To this day I still can recall each I attended before the age of 25. While I was still under the spell of youth and its self-denial of mortality, funerals and their accompanying emotions were strange and new.

Today, as I am moving through life with the spell of youth long broken, my appreciation of time continues to grow. No longer am I under the illusion time is forever, all its opportunities at my beck and call. Time is a tool that, if used properly, can be very rewarding. Underutilized, however, it can be a haunting reminder of opportunities offered, opportunities rebuffed.

I wish this lesson wasn't hidden from us in the days of our youth. Forever, I now realize, is a very long time.

"We should not view death as a period at the end of a sentence, but rather a comma leading us to a greater place." Although I believe deeply in the words spoken by Dr. Martin Luther King Jr., I still can't help hurting with each passing. Did I say everything I wanted to say to them? Did I make every effort to show them how much they meant to me? I'm not sure I can ever be fully satisfied, because these questions now are impossible to answer.

There appear to be several stages in this process. To a youth, the passing of a friend was a somewhat rare experience and many times the result of reckless living. Today I'm finding these passings more representative of the bedrocks of my early life. Time is now coming for the adults of my childhood. The next stage, one I am watching from the sidelines, is the passing of peers. This, I imagine, must be among the more painful of stages. These are not insulated by the stages of life, but rather represent our contemporary memories. I anticipate this to be a very difficult stage to manage.

Looking from the podium and across a modest chamber earlier this week, I recognized the faces of my childhood. The weekends at the lake, the holiday parties, the shared memories. I also saw the missing faces, the ones gone before the man whose life we celebrated that day.

If there is a lesson for me here, it is to every day look life straight in the eye and realize that the moments I let slip by, the opportunities missed, the words unspoken, will remain that way forever. I have to do the best I can to make the most of every moment with those I love. ●

6 New Family Member Shatters Alpha Image

Jack is a strange little guy. His body, measuring a thumb past 6-inches, obsessively magnetizes your attention regardless of his motion. His eyes, the odd blink, just plain freak me out.

I am not a lizard person.

Jack, our son's new Gecko, is an odd addition to our household. Arriving this past Christmas in a small plastic Tupperware-like container, I was not consulted – an action I am told was intentional.

Lizards creep me out. They are small, fast and project an unsettling confidence when looking at you. Furthermore, I'm pretty sure Jack thinks I'm a pretty tasty meal.

The first week my loving family called me up to my son's room. They'd just brought home a glass case complete with wood chips, a small water tray and half coconut shell for Jack to make his home inside.

Stepping in, I closed the door behind me.

"What's up?" I asked.

My wife, son and daughter, all on their hands and knees, turned my way.

"We need your help, we can't find Jack - he got out."

Suddenly, me towering over everyone in the room – and in theory the Alpha Male of the household – my body quickly groped for the door handle behind me. My feet, unbeknownst to me, were moving even faster.

With one foot out the door, my wife and kids couldn't keep a straight face any longer. I don't think they've ever laughed together any harder.

Regardless, I stand by my actions.

The past several weeks, however, are teaching me to face my fears. While I've always been a dog person – very comfortable with the mental makeup of canines – my newest experience just goes to show we're most likely to be scared by what we don't know. Jack, it turns out, is pretty much like the rest of the family. He likes his space and spends a great deal of time in his coconut. Periodically he'll come out to sun himself under the heat lamp or stroll around his grounds. I'm pretty sure if we'd put a tiny laptop in there he'd be surfing the web.

It is odd, as a fully-grown adult, parent, and husband, to admit I'd just as soon not share my space with a lizard. But Jack, in an unusual turn, is finding a place in our home.

Feeding time quickly became a spectator sport with everyone – sans me – gathering around to see the sacrificing of live crickets.

"You've got to see this," my wife told me, "he comes out of his shell whenever we lift the top of the cage. He knows what's going on."

One day I poked my head inside my son's bedroom door during the sacrificial event. Sure enough, out comes Jack as the crickets, happy to be out of the small plastic container, jump in dozens of directions. Jack moves to middle of his grounds and makes himself invisible by standing as still as a stone. And, just as everyone said, he lurches forward, the cricket disappearing faster than my eyes can process. After a few more morsels, Jack turns and confidently returns to his coconut.

Things are, however, thawing between us. Just last night I stepped into my son's room and lifted the lid of the cage. Out popped Jack. His eyes looking directly into mine, demonstrated a common understanding between us. I reached for the small container of crickets and dropped a few into his habitat. Jack, dutifully, moved like a skilled predator and dispatched of them quickly. And with his feeding over, we both turned to return to the comfort of our coconut shells – each with a better understanding of each other. ●

7 Remember to Say Thank You

As the National World War II Memorial in Washington, D.C. opens, I can't help but wonder about the very personal stories it represents – and the ones we'll never hear.

As a child, I walked among these proud and silent heroes long before I ever learned of their great personal sacrifices and the stories behind them.

"What is a SeaBee?"

I remember asking this question of my mother after noticing an odd bumper sticker on a neighbor's pickup truck. A strange bumblebee armed with a blazing machine gun, the logo easily captivated the mind of a 10-year-old.

My mother told me our neighbor had served with a special Navy branch that built things right in the middle of the war zone. Following the Marines into combat, the SeaBees built roads, bridges and hospitals. From the bumper sticker that captivated my attention, I now know my neighbor was one of the more than 325,000 individuals who bravely erected critical platforms for military operations. SeaBees, I learned, were literal in their claim: "We build, we fight."

Each week as my friends and I played baseball in the street we'd watch as our neighbor in his truck passed us by, a half-dozen fishing rods jostling between the seat and rear window, on the way to his favorite spot. No fanfare, no stories. Just quietly going through life like anyone else in my neighborhood.

I'm sorry to say I never knew enough to thank him at the

time.

Time is slipping away for us as a nation. I wonder how many more of these personal stories lived inside the modest homes of our neighborhood when we were children. I wonder how many of these experiences are lost to the footsteps of time.

My uncle, a veteran of the second world war, recently passed away. He spent the prime years of his life in the European theater, serving in the United States Navy. All I ever knew about his war experience was that he met my aunt overseas, sending for her when he returned home. Never did he speak of the sacrifices he made while a young man. Never did he bemoan or begrudge his service.

His favorite was story was not about battles and victories, but about how he couldn't seem to get his bride-to-be to America. Frustrated with red tape, back home in Kansas City, he shared with a close friend, "I've the most beautiful woman in the world and I can't get her home."

His friend relayed the story to an older woman with a government connection, someone whose small downtown business near hers had failed years before and forced him to change occupations. The woman offered to phone her friend to see if he could help, as he had relocated from Kansas City to Washington, D.C.

In fact, he had relocated to the White House. To the Oval Office, specifically.

That failed businessman – by then known as Mr. President – answered her call. Harry Truman reached out to a soldier he'd never met, quickly reuniting my uncle and his bride-to-be, and the tale of Truman's compassion has outlived them all.

You see, it is not the stories of battles I worry will be lost, but the very personal stories of those who served. The quiet -- but powerful -- side of human experience.

I only wish I'd known to say thank you. ●

8 Middle Age Angst Very Real

I didn't visit my grandmother enough before she died.

Sometimes events in our past – things we've not thought of in decades – oddly percolate to the top of our psyche and seemingly pull up a chair and sit for a while until we come to terms with our past.

I'm not sure my grandmother ever saw the north side of 5 feet – even with heels. Her heart, however, made up any shortage on the vertical side of the equation. I don't know if I've ever met a sweeter person – and I guess that is what hurts me the most today.

Being a teenager is pretty tough. You're always trying to navigate the world between adult and child – and not always with flying success.

"Can you come see your grandmother?" said the voice on the telephone.

I'm sixteen with a newly-minted driver's license in my pocket and with what seems millions of opportunities ahead of my high-mileage sedan and me.

"She's not doing well and it would really mean a great deal to her if you could come by to see her," said my grandmother's nurse.

I'm sure I came up with some sort of answer – careful not to pin myself down to a time or date. As a teenager with wheels, the unknown easily appealed to my sense of adventure. For some reason spending an afternoon with my frail grand-mother in her small apartment sharing hot tea, crackers and cheese, just didn't feel particularly compelling. Her apartment building, although clean and modern, smelled odd – almost as if someone had freshly made a pot of mothball soup and seasoned it with Pine Sol. The other residents were friendly, many carefully taking their hands from their aluminum walker to offer a warm wave as I strode past in what I now recognize as teenage arrogance.

I remember her apartment on the third floor with its small balcony and avocado green appliances.

My grandmother, well into her eighth decade, became increasingly frail with each visit. But today, I know it was not particularly her accelerating decline in health, but more my lack of visiting that amplified the withdrawals age demanded in exchange for another year of life.

I didn't visit enough and I didn't visit for the right reasons. I'm pretty sure I split my attention between her and the hands on my watch when I should've been listening. I know, considering my mother passed the summer before, these visits meant so much more than a teenage with keys in his pocket could ever understand. As a parent I now realize how someone can see the past by looking into the face of a child. The eyes, the twitches of the nose, the pace they use when speaking are commonly handed down from one generation to the next. We both hurt – but with a teenage heart I was looking to the future while she sat too many days alone in her apartment with-out a visitor.

Most times we realize too late to say we're sorry for it to matter. Other times, it takes decades to recognize we were wrong in the first place. The uncomfortable truth is, wisdom to understand our mistakes comes long past the time we can do anything about it to those we love. ●

9 The Incredible Shrinking World

"You know, I'm not particularly concerned about how my son's grades stack up against his classmates', let alone the rest of the school," I said. "My concern is, he needs to be equipped with the tools to successfully compete against a student sitting in a classroom in China today."

I still recall the patronizing look from the school administrator as I discussed educational expectations for my son, then in second grade. I wanted to stress that the quality of education, my son's preparation for life in a world of global competition, was much more important to me than anything else the school could offer. A solid, progressive education would be key to not only my son's — but every student's — future as the pool of competition expanded from their small classroom to places they had yet to find on a map.

Wow, did things move quickly.

I read a book in 1997 titled *The Death of Distance* by Frances Cairncross, which predicted the future of communications and its impact on our world. In it, the author laid out a world which is shrinking because of leaps in communication and efficiency. Business of the future would no longer follow the traditional tried and true models, Cairncross posed. Rather, it would make decisions based decreasingly on location and increasingly on capacity to communicate efficiently and effectively.

Location, Cairncross wrote, would no longer find itself at the empirical top of the list for many companies and the employment opportunities they provide. The impact of electronic transportation, for example, would transform the economics of moving information in ways few could imagine. Productivity could be gearing up for a boost of historical proportions.

Well, that day has arrived.

Today the buzzword is "outsourcing" — and it does not refer to competition between communities in nearby ZIP codes. Since the year 2000, an estimated 2.2 million jobs have disappeared from payrolls in the United States. Many of these jobs reflect structural changes not only to businesses but also to our national economy as it melts into the new global economy where ZIP codes are practically irrelevant. In today's world, the distance between the consumer and producer is measured by the speed of the broadband connection rather than the odometer on the delivery truck. Many of the jobs shed by the economy reflect monumental leaps in technology and currently do not — and may never again — exist. Therefore, we are witnessing an economy growing and expanding with the assistance of technological advances rather than recalling workers to their jobs.

As the world economy continues to educationally elevate itself, its inherently lower cost of living will feed the need of the bottom line as many corporations continue to search for ways to drive down expenses and increase top line revenues for favorable Wall Street opinions.

The growing criteria for prospective employees hinge more on educational background and abilities than on which ZIP code they return to at the end of their shifts. For example, today your medical data may be created around the corner from your home, electronically organized and manipulated in India, and then sent to another office in New York — all within a single business day.

This takes me back to the dark wooden desk separating me from the school administrator several years back. I know he doubted my forecast, my son competing against a student his age sitting in a classroom on the other side of the globe.

But then again no one — not even the highly acclaimed author of *The Death of Distance* — could have predicted the world changing overnight. ●

10 Farm Experience Connects Generations

My Uncle Albert owned the largest piece of machinery in the world. At least, it looked that way to the young boy looking up at the towering green combine tractor.

Growing up in a suburban neighborhood, I'd never set foot on a farm until a summer trip to the outskirts of southwestern Kansas to visit family. Located a couple miles north of Oklahoma and about the same distance east of Colorado, my uncle's farm opened my eyes to a world my family was a proud part of for generations.

"Time to get up," I heard one morning during my visit. Best I recall, it was still dark outside. Stumbling sleepily down the hallway, I made my way to the kitchen, where my aunt was racing around, fixing a breakfast big enough to feed my entire Little League baseball team back home.

As Uncle Albert reached for his morning coffee, I was reminded of how taken aback I had been at the size and strength of his hand when I shook it the night before. His palms and fingers were as tough as stone, but his touch was gentle, which I hadn't expected.

He sat at the table in his dark blue overalls, the brass buttons on the straps straining to keep his large body contained inside the denim. My uncle was a big man with a body built for rugged work. That body was designed not to fail, no matter what Mother Nature unleashed on any particular day.

After breakfast, my younger brother, Uncle Albert and I headed down a long dirt farm road with dust billowing behind us. From the rear window of the truck, it looked like we in a jet plane leaving vapor trails behind it as we raced across the sky above. The tall rows of corn lining the road added to the sensation of flying as we drove without a speed limit.

At one farm – there were several along the way – I stood in a field of corn for the first time, awestruck. The late July air weighed heavily in my lungs and I heard the scratching of the cornstalks as they attempted to catch any lost breeze that might have been wandering across the land.

"Come on in here, boys." My uncle's big voice easily covered the distance between us.

Coming in from the harsh light, my eyes had trouble adjusting to the quiet darkness around us. I discovered I was standing near tire so large it dwarfed everything around us. My uncle began climbing up a long ladder leading to a small compartment atop a gigantic, menacing machine, then extended a hand to us.

"Come on up boys," he said.

My brother and I opted for politeness, giving each other the "you first" nod to cover our unease at the ladder's height – and at where it might lead.

Moments later, curiosity having conquered fear, I found myself in the cab of a combine, looking out over a massive, rolling assembly of metal blades preparing for battle with the endless rows of corn that surrounded the barn. I was on top of the world, safely in the huge, gentle hands of my Uncle Albert, who was helping me claim an important part of my family history before it evaporated around us all. Sitting there, atop the largest machine I'd ever seen, my view of the world was forever changed.

Today, with fewer than two percent of the population directly active in farming, I know I'm not alone with my memories – or in my respect for the role farmers play in our daily lives.

Thank you, Uncle Albert -- and others -- for all you do for us. ●

11 Ceremonial Passing of the Keys

"Be careful," I say. And with barely any hesitation, my son puts the vehicle into gear, leaving me standing alone at the end of the driveway with a hole in my stomach.

For many of us, very few days carry as much significance as the day we turn over to our children the keys to the mower and the responsibility of maintaining the lawn.

OK, maybe I'm a bit sensitive, but the lawn has always been my baby, my domain, so to speak. Years of work, a culmination of extensive planning, work and tender loving care. Yes, I said love.

As my son makes a pass across the open lawn, I find myself reaching up to signal for him to slow down, kicking myself for not first putting him through a rigorous training program, sharing with him tips and knowledge only experience can bring. In lawn care, simple details can make all the difference. Knowing he, too, needs to learn from his experiences, I drop my hand to my side.

I start making a mental list of the gems of knowledge I'll need to pass on to him afterward. Does he know the slower he drives, the more time the blades repeatedly cross over the same piece of ground, making for a more uniformly cut surface? Does he know how to manage the metal shroud to within a half-inch of the concrete retaining walls to reduce the time I'll need to spend later with the weed eater? Should I tell him about the most time efficient routes around the yard? How about the classic "when in doubt, cut it high" rule (keeps weeds out, protects against excessive heat, etc.)? There are so many secrets I need to pass along.

I watch as he blazes alongside the house, the mower now running at full throttle. This, to him, is a race. The trail of grass blades spewing behind him reminds me of a scene out of "The Dukes of Hazzard." I severely doubt he has any consideration for achieving maximum uniformity of the cut.

Suddenly a strange feeling comes over me. I'm lost. There is nothing for me to do.

Sitting on the patio, watching as the mower continues to pass me by, I wonder if my days are numbered as the supreme commander of my lawn. If this works out, what will I do with all my free time?

Suddenly I hear a familiar voice behind me.

"Dad," my 9-year-old daughter says, "Do you want to go on a bike ride?"

And just as quickly, I realize that there are more important things for me to do than watch the grass grow. ●

12 Every Day is Father's Day

Every day, I now believe, is Father's Day. This thought came to my mind the other day driving home from the office, wondering who would be first me meet me at the door.

Pulling to a stop in the garage and unlocking my door, I feel a hand reach through the open driver's side window.

"First," my 9-year-old says, tagging me on the arm with her small hand as I open the door of my car.

As he is running up from the other end of the garage, I can hear my son groan, outfoxed by his younger sister.

Slowing to an amble, he tags me.

"First human," he says, agitating his sister.

"I'm a human — and I was first!"

So goes a daily competition. I hope it never ends.

Not to discount the idea of Father's Day, but to be honest, I find it redundant. Just waking up to having my children in my life makes every day special.

Not too many years ago I had no idea how empty my life was without children. Now seems like that was someone else's life, simple and uncomplicated. Time was mine to use — or waste — as I chose.

But then I became a family man and my life changed

forever. Never could I imagine the depth of emotion children could bring to my life. The humility is overwhelming and you find yourself wishing you could bathe in their waters forever.

The more I travel down this road of fatherhood, the more respect I have for those who've walked before me. Never did I understand or appreciate the incredible sacrifices they made on behalf of their children.

Once this feeling takes over there is absolutely nothing you wouldn't do to further your child's best interests in life. Material things are cheap substitutes for pleasure when compared with stopping the weed eater in mid-project to share a Popsicle on the back step with your child. There may be 24 hours in a day, but there is never enough time to spend one-on-one with your children. I find them so incredibly interesting, so alive. My son continues to grow as a young teenager, his questions forcing me to examine my own beliefs on subjects ranging from government censorship to entitlement programs to religious faith. As for my daughter, I'm convinced my name has never sounded more magical than when spoken to me by her. I am smitten in the fullest sense of the word.

Children are, I understand, blessings from God. To be a father is to become a caretaker of one of God's special creations. And although the responsibility is tremendous, the reward far outstrips anything a man can imagine.

So to me, Father's Day is not relegated to the third Sunday in June each year. Father's Day is, quite simply, every day I get to spend with my children. ●

13 Nature Comes Home

It was my 9-year-old daughter's first real lesson in nature. Only hours before, she and two neighbor boys raced into the garage as my son and I put away our golf clubs.

"Daddy, the cat has the baby rabbit!" she panted. "It ran into the woods across the street."

It was here I made my mistake.

"Well, if the cat has it, it's probably too late now."

From the looks on the faces of my daughter and her two younger friends, I could see my pragmatism was not just lost, but flat-out rejected.

I rethought my remark, actually embarrassed by my insensitivity.

Their eyes were still looking up to me for direction, completely ignoring my earlier comment.

"Well, maybe there is still time," I said, turning to my 13-year-old son.

As if reading my mind, he grabbed his seven-iron and ran back across the street with the younger kids leading him to where they last saw the cat disappear with the baby rabbit.

Minutes later the four of them were back in the garage, the tiny rabbit cupped in my daughter's small hands.

"Do you think it's going to be okay?" she said.

I could sense the despair, despite her firm and controlled voice.

Reaching out, I took the animal into my hand, its entire body dwarfed by my palm. I could not recognize any evidence of breathing or response, although the rabbit appeared unharmed.

"I'm not sure," I said, couching my words. "Let's let him rest."

Reaching over to my work bench, I cleared out a planting basket, laying down several layers of papers towels for bedding. She placed the rabbit into its bed and set it on the garage floor. The kids circled around, watching for signs of life.

After a few minutes passed, I suggested we let the rabbit rest so they could come back and check on it later. Agreeing, they all ran back across the street to play on a swing set.

Looking down at the tiny ball of fur, I again felt guilty about my cold remarks earlier, knowing the children were following their hearts, me my mind.

Several hours later I came back into the garage to find my daughter riding circles alone on her bike.

Without stopping, she shared her prognosis without emotion.

"The rabbit is dead."

She'd apparently been keeping an eye on the rabbit while everyone else was outside, and she had reached her conclusion about its fate.

I walked over to her and put my arm around her.

"We'll bury the rabbit in the morning, okay?" I said.

She looked down at the rabbit again and behind her strong front, I could see a touch of the sadness she held back.

The next morning we walked together to a quiet spot behind the house and dug a small hole. She insisted the rabbit be placed in an empty stapler box for burial.

She helped replace the dirt, we said a few words over the tiny rabbit, and we returned to the house, both of us having grown from the experience. ●

14 Fingertips Replace Spoken Words

The world is quickly changing at the end of my fingertips.

This past week, while away from home for a couple days, I found myself talking with both my teenagers at the same time – although they weren't even in the same room.

A couple years ago I'd have dialed an area code and then a local phone number at the end of the day to tell them good night. We'd each take time to talk briefly about the day as they'd pass the phone to the other. Today, however, we talk without ever hearing each other's voices – through the magic of text messaging. While my wife and I still 'old school' communicate on the phone, our kids are moving to a communication model in which their cell phone is less a tool for speaking and rather one employed for texting cryptic messages back and forth.

"miss u" I type into the tiny keyboard on my cell phone, all in lower case.

Looking at the screen I realize my spelling is also taking a turn – as if I'm learning a brand-new language from my children. Vowels are becoming optional, left behind like extra baggage on a long cross-country drive.

I touch the send key and the message evaporates from the screen and I then begin another message – this time to my son.

"hey u", I write.

Before I can touch the send button again my phone registers an incoming message from my daughter.

After a quick reply I soon find myself 'speaking' with both of them at the same time although I can picture them in different parts of the house back home.

While not the same as a phone call, this is their chosen method of communication – and one I'm willing to actively participate in order to remain a part of their lives. Change is natural and sometimes it requires us to understand we can't just sit along the sidelines and let the world change around us without adapting. So in the past year I've learned to meet my teenagers on their own ground – even if that means speaking with my fingertips.

Another message comes in from my son– and soon another on top of it sent from my daughter. For the next few minutes I find myself in a flurry of activity reading and responding to the incoming messages. While the number of words used in our conversations is limited, my imagination is painting a picture of each of them sitting in their rooms staring into the tiny screens balanced between their fingers.

I like our new world of communicating. It is brief, instant and to the point. In fact, it is a very efficient and effective method of sharing thoughts between each of us.

My fingertips type out my "good night" and hesitantly touch the send button.

Oddly enough, although this new experience is light years from reading a bedtime story as they go to sleep, I'm okay with the new world. I know now they're always as close as the end of my fingertips. ●

15 Family Lore: Stories Not To Pass Down

It's not my fault my wife won't let me fix too many things around the house. Apparently the "training" my brother and I had as children scares the daylights out of her.

Sitting at the dinner table the other night, I shared with the kids how my dad invented surround sound for the television in our home decades before it hit the mass market.

"How'd he do that?' my son asked, suddenly interested.

"Well," I said, "One time when he was fixing the television..."

"How do you fix a television?" he interrupted, fascinated.

"Whenever the television would break, my dad had this big cardboard box of transistor tubes in the basement he'd bring up and…"

"Tubes?" my son asked. "What is a tube?"

"Televisions were filled with dozens of these big vacuum tubes, about the size of salt and pepper shakers, that needed to be replaced when the picture or sound went crazy."

That satisfied him.

"What about surround sound?" he prompted.

"My dad was always fiddling with this television," I continued. "Our house never saw a television repairman. Sometimes my brother and I would come into the living room and find my mom's makeup mirrors strategically arranged around the room and my dad peeking out from behind the television."

"How's the red, son?" my dad would say.

Never were my brother or I allowed behind to see just what he was doing back there. No explanations, no instructions. Just... magic.

"Fine." I'd answer. After all, red is red when you're 9 years old.

Next we'd hear some mumbling, then some rustling and clinking from his box of tubes. It always reminded us of the professor in "The Wizard of Oz."

So one time the sound went out on the television and next thing we knew, up in the living room we found the professor and his box of magical tubes. Only this time -- after several trips to Radio Shack for new tubes -- he couldn't figure it out. Drove him nuts, his being an electrical engineer and all.

A couple days passed and again my brother and I walked into the living room to find an old television from the basement sitting on the opposite side of the living room, hidden behind the main chairs.

"Dad," we asked, "How's this work?"

With a gleam in his eye he explained his breakthrough and how we were to operate his new system.

"Well," he said, "The one in the basement, the picture is shot, so I brought it up. That darn sound problem in the other, well, I just can't figure it out yet. So here's the plan for now: Whenever you boys are watching television, just make sure you then reach around the chair and turn the channel on the other television, too."

My son let out a long, disappointed sigh. I think he truly expected to hear how his grandfather had actually invented surround sound. (We were talking major bragging rights for a teenager.)

As I reached for my drink at the dinner table I caught my wife's eye and got the distinct feeling that maybe, just maybe, some family stories should not be passed down after all. ●

16 Don't Think, Just Throw

"Now don't just slap this putt," I said to my 13-year-old son earlier this week while we were playing golf.

His shot rested five feet from the flag on a par-3 hole, presenting him with his first-ever birdie opportunity in a career which had begun just that summer.

Knowing the rarity of such an opportunity, I reminded him once again to take his time.

"You need to read the green first and have a plan," I said.

"I already have a plan," he said, confidently placing the putter head next to the small white ball. "I plan to put the ball into the cup."

I watched as his ball slammed into the back of the cup – just as he planned -- besting my score for the hole as well.

Sometimes I marvel at the confidence – or is it lack of fear? – our children exhibit in situations that routinely intimidate us as adults. Why is it we, supposedly the mature and rational ones, seem to be able to rattle ourselves? With the wealth of knowledge we've supposedly acquired through life's experiences, why do we tend to think ourselves out of opportunities, and therefore, chances for success?

I'm reminded of a scene out of the movie *Bull Durham* in which a young pitcher is given explicit instructions by a road-smart catcher on how to be successful with his amazingly talented arm: "Don't think, just throw." I find myself coming back to this phrase when faced with new challenges, ignoring the little voice of wisdom inside.

Recently I had the opportunity to play golf with an amazingly talented teenage golfer who'd just returned from the state high school tournament, and I quickly learned what separated him from the rest of our party of casual golfers. Gathered on the putting green, our group needed to select a single putt from where our team would putt. As the three of us adults spent a couple minutes trying to debating between two choices, neither more than seven feet from the hole, I noticed our high school golfer was a bit disinterested in the whole process.

"Which putt do you prefer?" I asked.

"It doesn't matter," he responded politely, "We're going to make either putt anyway."

To his seasoned partners, the putt might not drop for many reasons. Experience tells us we've probably missed that putt a hundred times before he was even born. The little voice in each of was thumping its fist on piles of supporting documentation in our heads.

In the end, with his confidence flowing through us, we ignored our little voices and slammed the putt down.

As we walked off the green, a team member turned to me and said, "Now we know why he plays on a completely different level than the rest of us."

So this summer, my son and this talented young golfer have taught me that the best way to defeat the little voice inside us is to simply remember: "Don't think, just throw." ●

17 The Gift of Friendship

Ten years seemed like 10 minutes — that is, except for the three children joining us around the table at a restaurant earlier this week.

A decade after losing track of a good friend and his wife, I found a listing of their last name on an Internet search engine. The initials matched his and his wife's, so I picked up the telephone.

As the phone rang on the other end, I began to wonder where I would start. How do I explain I couldn't keep track of two very important people — both of whom stood with my wife and me at our wedding — when we finally met again?

By the third ring, I was out of time.

"Hello?" came a somewhat familiar voice.

"Brian?" I asked

"Yes," he replied with a hint of reservation.

Not sure how to begin, I resorted to blurting out my name, reintroducing myself to the party on the other end of the line.

A pause on the other end was followed by a deep, warm laugh — one I'd missed for a decade. Instantly, the years between us evaporated.

We found ourselves talking as if we'd just been at each

others' homes the weekend before. Only this conversation revealed we had daughters about the same age. He'd met my son, now 13 years old, only a couple of times before our careers and new lives caused us to lose track of each other.

We spoke for nearly 10 minutes. I told him we were traveling to his city for a couple of days and would love to get together for dinner with him and his family. And, just like old times, we'd also manage to squeeze a golf game into the plans. Only this time we'd have a new player along. My son would be joining us.

Life has a way of getting away from you if you're not careful.

Good friends are very hard to come by. They are, I'm learning, born not out of convenience, but an honest respect for the other person — warts and all. In other words, love.

As I find my world continuously evolving around me — children, career, new interests — I find myself with a stronger appreciation for true friendship. Someone once told me in life you'll have dozens of acquaintances but only a small handful of real friends. And to me, the words ring more true with each passing year.

True friendship is a gift from one person to another and should never be taken lightly. A friend sees you for who you really are on the inside, not just the person you present on the outside. Odds are, they've seen you at your best and worst, yet accept you all the same. They couldn't care less who you think you are. They know the real you and will tell you in a heartbeat to your face — like it or not.

God blesses us with both family and friends. One is by blood, the other by the generosity of the heart. And as I rediscovered around the table earlier this week, great gifts only get better with time. ●

18 Dressed for a Brave New World

I look good with my toenails painted bright red ... so says my 7-year-old daughter. There is something very unusual about the relationship between a father and daughter, something my wife began warning me about right after our daughter's birth.

Knowing I grew up in a household where dinners were not complete without generous servings of ketchup, mustard and testosterone, my wife knew I would be embarking on a most unfamiliar and dangerous journey.

You see, my brother never painted my toenails while I slept in front of the television.

Where he and I would build rickety wings from the remains of our old kites, jumping from the top of an old doghouse attempting to fly, my daughter prefers to "play."

"Dad," she asked me earlier this week, "can you slay dragons?"

"What?" I said, noting the mischievous look in her eyes.

"Since Mom is gone to the store, let's go into the other room," she said. "I'll play the princess trapped in a tower and you can slay the dragon and rescue me."

Without waiting for my answer, she raced down the hall and climbed up into a large overstuffed chair, expecting me to rescue her from an imaginary dragon.

These things just never happened growing up with my brother.

Walking down the hall, I began to wonder how I had managed to live the majority of my life absent of such an experience. Also, what tool I needed to slay the dragon lurking below the red chair.

Squinting as to appear asleep, she pointed to an old, broken badminton racquet conveniently lying on the floor.

"Use that," she advised. "It's your sword."

As I approached the imaginary dragon, quickly slaying it and rescuing the princess, I couldn't help smiling at my wife's prophetic words.

Over the past several years, she has enjoyed these strange detours our daughter leads me on, knowing how out of my environment I really feel, but also how fully willing I am to make my daughter happy. Together we've choreographed a special dance of spins and twirls, worked out special hand signals, and created certain telling looks reserved only for each other.

"There is never anything as special as the relationship between a little girl and her father," my wife tells me repeatedly, a reflection of her love for and dedication to her own father.

But I am learning I am not alone in the brave new world into which my daughter is luring me.

A few days after waking up and finding my toenails painted a bright red, I was changing for a game of golf with a group of old friends. As I began switching socks, someone noticed my new fashion statement.

"You know," he said, "my daughter painted my fingernails green the other day ... and I never resisted. How in the world does this happen to us?"

I smiled, appreciating how I was not alone in this world where men wear painted toenails and slay dragons for trapped princesses. ●

19 A Different Mid-Life Crisis

I'm having a mid-life crisis, but it's not one I ever expected.

"What size is that shirt he's wearing?" I ask as our 13-year-old son walks past my wife and me, the shoulders of his tee-shirt straining around his growing frame.

"An adult small," she says. "And we just bought it in the spring."

It is now not too uncommon for me to find his socks and shirts accidentally mixed in with mine, fooling even me at times. I guess I always knew this day would come, so it was what I heard next that actually knocked the wind out of me.

"Did you know," my wife said, "that your 9-year-old daughter is now shopping for -- and fitting in -- clothes from the teen department?"

I could feel the blood drain from my face. I am not ready for this. And I'm not talking about the new back-to-school fashion styles. The end of the innocence is approaching.

For as long as I can remember, the phrase "we've two young children" has been rolling off my tongue. But lately I'm realizing this particular combination of words is outdated. Our children, I'm now recognizing, are about halfway through the traditional window of living under the roof of our home. My son, as a young teenager, will most likely be off to college before a common car loan could be paid off. And his sister is single-digit years from her anticipated launch into the real world.

For years, people have told me time accelerates the older you get, something I believed to be an overexaggeration. Only now I find myself uttering this same piece of advice to others with small children.

Apparently a middle-age crisis is not limited to the birth date on my driver's license. I can clearly see the days ahead with our children as limited, something that never crossed my mind while I held them in my arms as infants. Then, with only a few days behind us, the future was without a horizon. Now, out of nowhere, I am beginning to see the first hints of the sunset and my heart is painfully panging back at me.

The other night while our family was out to dinner, a young couple came into the restaurant, sliding into the booth side by side. After their dinner arrived, they spoke long and uninterrupted to each other.

"Gee," my wife said, "remember days of sitting on the same side of the booth without negotiating with the kids first?"

I smiled, looking over at the couple, remembering the days she was referring to.

A short while later as we walked across the parking lot to our car, my wife reached down and took my hand. Our conversation returned to the young couple inside the restaurant.

"You know," she said watching my mid-life crises walking ahead of us, "I remember those days, but I would not trade them for anything now."

With help like that, I just might make it through this after all. ●

20 Don't Phone Home

A silent, powerful coup recently occurred in our home.

Last week while I was standing in the kitchen, the telephone began to ring. Leaning against the counter, I did not flinch, nor did my wife look up from the magazine she was reading at the table.

Before the second ring could be completed, feet could be heard racing across the upstairs to floor.

You see, the telephone is no longer for us.

More and more we find our 9-year old cuddled up with the telephone, chatting with one of her friends. And now our son is a teenager, so keeping track of who called when and why is pretty much a lost cause. (Thank goodness for Caller ID.)

How does this happen? Not too long ago if the telephone rang, it was for either my wife or me. Save telemarketers - who can pinpoint the most inopportune times - the caller usually was a good friend, a family member, or someone from the office. But now, things are upside down.

I remember how strange it first felt when a voice on the other line asked to speak with my daughter. It was as if I was turning over the steering wheel while driving down the interstate. Little did I know how close I was in my thinking.

Last I checked - according to the directory - the telephone

still is in my wife's and my name. As a matter of fact, she is the one who pays the bill each month. But calls are rarely for either of us.

I can't say this happened overnight, but it did occur silently. I think the frequency of calls and us asking the party to hold while we searched for the child of interest became too much work. Eventually, we began to recognize that the statistical percentages of calls were no longer for us, and if we waited long enough one of the kids would answer it.

It did take some adjusting. Much as with Pavlov's dogs, the ringing of a telephone used to provoke from me an involuntary impulse to answer it. That is, until recently. These days, after proper training, I can patiently let the telephone ring three, maybe four times, without feeling compelled to answer it. With our children in charge it's almost like having living, breathing answering machines walking around in the house. Only these answering machines eat lots of food, drink large amounts of pop and plan to go to college.

And there is another side I'm beginning to recognize. That is, I long for the good old days when I could easily reach my wife on the telephone. Yesterday I phoned to tell her I'd be late coming home.

"Hello?" said a soft voice on the other side of the line. It wasn't my wife.

"Hi, sweetie," I said to my daughter.

We began to talk about what she did during the day. Many minutes later, I realized I'd forgotten who and why I'd called in the first place.

I guess the phone isn't for either my wife or me, after all.●

21 Little Girls are Still Big Girls Inside

Despite his worn edges, drooping ears and faded brown fur, Baby Growler will always hold a special place in my heart.

For my daughter, now 9 years old, he may be out of sight, but he's not out of mind.

It's strange how children — even adults — emotionally grab hold of an inanimate object and project emotions only they can see and feel.

And so it goes with this stuffed animal and my daughter.

Shortly after Baby Growler came into our family, years ago, my daughter awakened my wife and me in the middle of the night with tears rolling down her cheeks.

"What's the matter, sweetie?" my wife asked.

"I can't find Baby Growler," she said between sniffles.

Struggling to wake, I forced my feet onto the floor.

Minutes later, after a quick midnight tour of her room — which included a peek beneath her bed, inside her closet and into the piles of other stuffed animals relegated to second-tier status — I found myself outside in the cold, looking through our car to see if he'd slipped between the seats.

After doing the best I could do in my sleep-induced fog, I came back in the house empty handed to find our daughter curled up beside my wife in our bed. The next morning, my daughter's missing friend was discovered resting beside her bed, once again proving I'm probably not the person to call in the middle of the night for the answer to a Jeopardy question.

Fast-forward nearly a half-dozen years to yesterday. Our daughter, now growing up in ways not easily measured with a pencil mark on the inside of a door frame, decided it was time for her to get her ears pierced. After months of deliberation, which included a couple of dry runs to watch other people get their ears pierced, she finally felt comfortable with the prospect.

"Guess what?" she said the night before at dinner.

"I give up. What?" I said.

"I'm going to get my ears pierced before school starts this year."

Knowing her track record — my having accompanied her on a dry run — I wasn't sure where she was getting her extra courage.

The next day, I watched as my wife and daughter came through the front door of my office. With a smirk, the "got-cha" look my daughter seems to have made a her signature, she walked toward me.

I could see small gold posts seated in each earlobe and a proud grin spreading across her face. I admired her for the manner in which she worked up the courage to have this procedure done. This was her decision, her call. She, no matter how I feel, is growing up.

Then I glanced down, only to see Baby Growler in her arms, a rare public field trip for him these days.

She may be growing up, but inside, my daughter still is the little girl who woke me up to find her lost friend so many years ago. ●

22 Night Sky Twinkle Magic

"Look," my 9-year-old daughter said the other night. "Is that the star you said is really a planet?"

Walking out from the garage, I see she's stopped her bicycle at the end of the driveway in front of our home. In the western sky, the sun finally lets go of its final rays of light. Brilliant red fades into a dark absence of light. I walk down to join her.

I look up at single beacon of white light — a pinprick in a black wall — occupying nearly the exact spot the sun had occupied an hour before.

"Yes, it is. Why?" I said.

With the light from the garage spilling out toward us, she gets off her bike and stands next to me.   With each passing day I marvel at her progress beyond the physical. Increasingly, her questions have become deeper, more difficult for me to answer.

"How do you know the difference?" she said.

"The twinkle."

"The what?"

"The twinkle. If you look closely and you can see some twinkling, it's generally a star and not a planet."

Looking down I notice she's giving me one of her patented looks. It says, "Okay, now tell me the real story."

Trying not to make this a science project, I hold back on a long-winded explanation of space dust, or distance measured in light years between galaxies — all contributing factors in the twinkling illusion she sees as we stand at the end of the driveway. But in the near-decade we've been together, I've learned she is not interested in the details behind the illusion. She is only interested in the magic.

We stand together as the dark sky seemingly expands around us, bringing more samples to analyze. Taking turns, we are trying to identify planets from stars with our twinkling method when a cool summer breeze sweeps past us.

She turns and looks back at the bright light, now floating above our neighbor's blue spruce tree, that caught her attention earlier.

Fiddling with the pedals on her bike, she looks back up at me.

"Can I still make a wish on a planet?"

"Well," I said, "I don't see why not. Do you want to?"

"I kind of already did."

"So what do you think?" I said. "Do you think it'll work?"

She smiles, getting back on her bike for one last loop around the driveway.

"Yes."

Watching her ride toward the light of the garage at that moment, so do I. ●

23 Shopping a Sport?

Nothing personal to my brother, but raising my daughter would be a lot easier if he were my sister.

Last Saturday, sitting on the sofa in the middle of my early morning ritual of coffee and ESPN's SportsCenter, I heard footsteps behind me.

"We're ready."

Turning around, I discovered my 9-year-old daughter and her friend standing in the kitchen. One look at their outfits -- skirts and boots complete with matching handbags -- and I knew I was already in for much more than I had bargained for.

The night before, when my wife asked me if I'd watch the girls while she went out with a friend, it I figured the girls would sleep late and maybe eventually want to ride around the block on their bikes. I'd have coffee, catch up on the baseball scores from the night before, and it'd be an easy assignment.

"Ready?" I asked, confused.

"We're going shopping, right?" she said.

Apparently, my morning was over and I was to be a chauffeur for two girls who considered shopping an extracurricular activity akin to a sport. Growing up, I can honestly say, this was one event in which my brother and I never participated.

The girls and I found ourselves at a restored 100-year-old barn, where a huge community shopping opportunity had been created. As I pulled into a parking spot in the middle of someone's yard, a strange fever seemed to sweep over the girls. Suddenly, their speech patterns raced and they frantically fumbled to find the door latches and unbuckle their seat belts. We began to walk (Correction: I walked, they raced) toward the dozens of white vendor tents surrounding the tall, red barn. A live folk band's gospel music drifted alongside the aroma of elephant ears cooking inside a small trailer.

I was relegated to chauffeur status, comfortably trailing behind the girls as they bounced between tables of handmade jewelry, stuffed animals and candles. I think they touched just about everything, constantly looking into their small handbags to count out dollar bills and change.

Then the strangest thing happened. They ran out of money, but they didn't stop shopping. This concept, promise, is completely foreign to most males. Out of money is pretty much game over -- or so I thought.

As the sun began to heat up the morning, the girls retraced their steps as if they'd missed something. My mind kept wandering to all the nice things we could be doing that did not involve shopping. Riding bikes, for instance, or maybe playing a game of Whiffle ball. But as the hours rolled on I began to notice something different, something beyond the shopping.

The girls were working the crowd, running up to friends and saying hello, showing their catch for the day. This shopping trip, I began to realize, was not just rummaging through tables and booths, but a great big social event. The girls seemed to bloom and revel in the environment, a world completely unknown to my brother and me as kids.

Who know? Maybe next time he and I are together, I can casually toss out the idea of going shopping and he'll eagerly accept the opportunity.

Yeah. Sure. ●

24 Time Altered by Unknown

Years can whisk by like the cars of a freight train gathering speed, each month and year rushing by faster and faster until you feel as if you are merely a spectator along the tracks.

That familiar spectator role in no way prepared me for experiencing the absolute opposite with our teenage son recently. His driver's license not even a year old, he didn't come home at his usual time and in not doing so introduced me to a brand-new measurement of time. It was one where minutes felt like hours, one amplified by the onset of sunset.

I'd been working in the basement, expecting the garage door to open at any minute. It's funny how you have these self-imposed deadlines, developing a feel for certain things. Our son's regular schedule consisted of going to school, staying for cross-county practice and being home by 5:30 p.m., give or take 15 minutes. I could pretty much set my watch by him, until a recent Tuesday.

I noticed he was late.

"Did he call you?" I asked my wife.

"No," she said. "You?"

He hadn't called me, either. Had we missed something on the calendar? A quick check -- no cross-country meet on the schedule. We began racking our brains for clues and tried to give him the benefit of a doubt, but a full half-hour had ticked away by this time.

"I think I'll call his cell," I said.

His voice mail picked up.

"Hey," I said, trying to remain calm. "Just looking for you. Dinner will be ready soon. Give us a call."

Another 10 minutes passed. He hadn't returned my call and the garage door stayed tightly closed, and I could feel fear begin to creep over me. This was very unlike him. We've always kept in close touch with each other, even if we were just running next door for a few minutes. Like any teenager, his cell phone might was like an appendage. So why didn't he pick up? It didn't feel right.

The sun's descent accelerated, and what I normally considered a benign nightly event suddenly felt like a threat.

Forty-five minutes late, and it felt like a week had passed. I reached for my cell phone again, just to make sure I hadn't somehow missed his call. It had been 10 minutes since I'd left him a voice mail, and I found myself anxiously leaving him another. Five minutes later, a third.

Ninety minutes later, the garage door opened and a strange, cleansing wave of relief washed across me. He'd called a few minutes earlier to let us know he was at his coach's house, helping build a homecoming float for the next day's parade. He called from a friend's cell phone. His had been in the passenger seat of his car the whole time.

As a parent, the unknown is the most terrifying thing about being apart from your child. Possibilities you'd never normally entertain begin to take over your mind, and you find yourself looking for clues you may have overlooked. You mostly expect a positive outcome. But it's a cruel trick when anxiety enters the equation and painfully twists your perspective, turning the familiar into something you don't even recognize. Time seems to slow to a crawl, even while it's racing by

Thankfully, when that garage door opened, time in my world was instantly restored to its rightful balance of 60 seconds to the minute. ●

25 New Son Reawakens Deep Emotions

Sometimes the most powerful words are those never spoken. It's not so much unwillingness, but rather that we discover words are surprisingly inadequate when deep emotions are in play. And so it was with a first-time father carrying his newborn son against his chest in a small restaurant I recently visited in western Georgia.

Proudly holding his young son against his jacket, gently swaying to a gentle rhythm only he and his son could hear, the father's eyes spoke volumes of love words could never hope to capture and share.

Grasping toward our voices, the baby's hands reached outward as tiny fingers closed in the empty air surrounding him.

"He's almost two months old," said the father, "and nearly 13 pounds."

The vitals, much like the reverse side of a baseball trading card, quickly become — and remain — the key component of communication with other parents. Most any parent can recall the length and weight of their children with more accuracy than they can their own Social Security numbers.

The full head of black hair, starkly outlined against his father's white coat, amplified the connection between this father and son.

As my hand reached forward toward the small fingers, my mind raced in reverse to a time when my children comfortably rested in my arms. Never did I feel as proud. And without a doubt, I recognized the very same emotion in the eyes of the new father.

Soon he and his son found themselves fielding attention from others in the restaurant. Nothing draws a crowd like a new baby, and with good reason. As I've learned, each child is a blessing and the natural attraction never wanes.

My thoughts again returned to the first time I set eyes on my son, and the stirring power I felt charge through my body. If up to that moment I'd ever questioned the meaning of life, the answer was now boldly gasping his first breaths of air before me in the hospital maternity room. Although 13 years now separate me from that introduction to my son, the moment is still as vivid as a conversation I had an hour ago.

Feeling the young boy in the restaurant anchor his surprisingly strong hand around my finger, I looked back up at the father while he smiled and answered questions from another passer-by. His face was totally aglow in love and pride, a special expression a parent can easily recognize.

It was then I began to suspect I might not be alone in my feelings.

Looking around at the others who took turns adoring the young boy resting on his father's chest, I began to recognize they too probably felt a powerful reawakening of the very emotions I discovered resurfacing inside me. At that moment, I believe we too could hear the comforting and familiar rhythm the father and young son danced to on the restaurant floor that evening. ●

26 Genetics Play Role in New Sound

Long ago, scientists began to point to genetics as a contributor to our species' evolution.

As parents, we get a front row seat to the show. With each birth comes the search to discover us in our children, be it the color of the hair, the shape of the hand or an oversized big toe passed down for generations. But I'm thinking scientists might be overlooking an entire strain of genes coming to the surface in my 13-year-old son and his reaction to cars.

My wife first began to recognize signs of this peculiar phenomenon within the past year.

"It's a guttural sound," she said, telling me of his reaction a couple of days ago when they drove past a local car dealership with a brand-new Ford Mustang GT on display. "It seems to start low in his stomach and just build to the top. It really seems to be involuntary and he's oblivious to everything else at the time."

The sound she describes — one I know all too well — manifests itself in a release of a deep, powerful version of "whoa." Proper enunciation cues are a long, drawn out, almost rolling sound before fading out due to a complete exhausting of air in the lungs causes the sound to fade away.

This, as a father, makes me very proud. You see, unlike the blue eyes and blonde hair that came from his mother, this special gene came from the male chromosome found inside me

— a result of growing up in a small town of muscle car-crazy gearheads. Cars were separated into two categories: muscle cars and "What can we do to it to make it louder and faster?"

As a childhood friend of mine said recently, "It was a town where even the girls knew how to switch out a carburetor on a Friday night." To this day I am still known, when pulling up to a particular favorite model of muscle car, to turn off the CD and gently roll down the window just to listen to the looping sound of a high-lift cam, belching air rolling out the back of a free-flow dual exhaust, and the undeniable sound of a large block V-8 engine. In many ways, to those of us with this affliction, it is like drinking from the fountain of youth.

But with my son, honestly, I was very worried several years ago after a trip to the Chicago Auto show. It's not that he wasn't excited about all the cars — he was. But it was the types of cars he was interested in that scared me the most: cars loaded with flashy electronics, dual-fuel engines, dashboards that changed colors with the driver's mood -- all while playing music to fit the individual driver's taste. I felt as if maybe, just maybe, the Nintendo generation might be immune to horsepower. Make that lots and lots of horsepower.

For the next several hours, I took him around to show him large V-8 and V-12 motors, explained how to read the spec sheets for horsepower ratings and sprinkled in bits of racing history only to have him ask me at one point, "What is the point of having all this horsepower if you can't use it?" I'll never forget the painful wound he inflicted with those words, or my stark realization I just might be the last of a dying breed.

But nature is a grand and mysterious thing. In its wisdom, the "automotive gene" began to rise to the surface in our teenage son, as my wife has witnessed. Today, he and I share an instinctive respect for a low rumbling V-8, an appreciation for aggressive sheet metal design and the uncompromising need for a manual transmission.

That, and an involuntary guttural sound passed down through generations. ●

27 Traveling Family Style Pays Dividends

Last week I spent 1,224 round-trip miles driving along the rain and snow-blown Midwestern interstates, cooped up with my wife and our two children. 11 hours each way. And I wouldn't trade it for the world.

"So are you going out of town for Thanksgiving?" asked a co-worker early last week.

"Yes," I said, mentioning we'd be going back to my home-town to visit family. "And we're driving."

I could see a look of dread roll across the person's face, even though I was the one traveling.

"With two kids — you're driving — 11 hours? Each way? Better you than me," he said pityingly.

A lot of life is how we look at it. I believe I'm not too unlike many of you reading this today. Our lives are pretty full, yet the one thing most of us ache for is more time with our family. Daily life has a way of unconsciously forcing us into a quiet rhythm. Get up in the morning and go to work. Come home. Eat dinner. Supervise homework. Sort the mail. Go to bed. Next day, well…repeat.

How much time do we really get to spend with our fami-lies — one-on-one? Last week I was reminded why I've always loved long road trips with them. Everyone can tell about their personal horror stories (the fuel-injection system freezing in the middle of a snow storm while crossing the Appalachian Mountains with a newborn in the back seat comes to mind) but we don't seem to tell how we, confined in a relatively small place for an extended time, can be reminded how much we love to be around those in our life.

Although my wife and I generally toss an armload of CD's onto the floorboard before pulling out of the driveway, we rarely play more than a couple, spending most of the time with the stereo off and talking for hundreds of miles. I can honestly say my wife and I really look forward to these long trips to get reacquainted. Our conversations flow without structure or direction. And before we know it, we've covered many miles-- even more distance in conversation.

There is a wonderful intimacy to these trips, due in part to the close confines for an extended period of time. Considering the time constraints many of us find ourselves in today, I often wonder how much time and attention this would translate into in our normal world. How many days of squeezing a few minutes of conversation between the kids going down for the night and us hitting the lights would it take to equal our highway time?

As for our kids, each long trip reminds us how much they've matured right in front of our eyes and that we really may not have recognized it, blinded by the intense light of our daily lives. For example, no longer are our stops strategically arranged by restaurants with a playground to burn off energy. And in a bittersweet way, it makes me sad. Another stage is now behind us forever.

There is an old saying: "Success is not a destination but a journey." As someone who finds the discoveries inside the car more interesting than anything along the roadside, I agree. ●

28   'In Santa We Trust'?

Are we on the cusp of becoming a godless nation? Depending on your point of view, recent events and rulings could lead to a completely different nation in the near future.

"Hey," my 13-year-old son protested, sitting next to me as we watched an episode of a popular television show, "They can't have a crucifix up in a classroom."

I paused, looking more closely at the screen. In the background, a small, wooden crucifix hung from the wall next to the green chalkboard in the classroom. It wasn't that the crucifix was displayed in the sitcom classroom that caught my attention, but his instant recognition that the display of religious items in a public school is a violation of accepted political correctness. His generation has been conditioned to be on the watch for any crossing of the line between religion and public space.

This is a strange and troubling irony for a country identifying itself as "one nation, under God."

For a nation founded on the principles of freedom – primarily, freedom of religion -- are we now becoming conditioned to feel shame for our religious beliefs? Mankind, science supports, is a spiritual being. But today, we find a growing effort to reverse this ingrained and deeply held value in every aspect of our lives. It would seem as if the goal of this driving force is to neutralize any public expression of religion, purging it from the public psyche.

The United States is an amazing collection of diverse religious beliefs and organizations. The American Religious Identification Survey, a 2001 study by The Graduate Center of the City University of New York, contends that 81 percent of American adults identify themselves with a specific religion. Furthermore, a USA/Gallup poll (2002-Jan) identified 50 percent of respondents as "religious" and another 33 percent as "spiritual but not religious." Granted, there is a shift among the religious categories, but the underlying theme of the recognition of a "God" is undeniable. Imagine the support a candidate who receives more than 80 percent of the vote would enjoy. Who could contest it?

By contrast, take a look at the attempt to eradicate any religious reference from our daily lives. God is no longer welcome in public schools. Mere mention is enough to create a national media fire storm. Basic respect for the entire holiday season -- which encompasses observances of significant events by a majority of religions -- is now being sanitized. Schools across the nation change the term "Christmas vacation" to "winter vacation," as if this little dance with words can erase the single most recognized holiday in our nation. Seventy-six percent of the subjects in the American Religious Identification Survey classify themselves as Christians, after all. This push, if successful, will contribute to a society with an instinct to prohibit any type of religious message by any organization, eradicating a founding principle of our nation.

They say there are no atheists in foxholes. If we're not careful, someday the only person anyone will recognize during the holiday season will be the big guy in the red and white suit. I may believe in magic, but I'm not banking on going to the North Pole after my days on earth are complete. ●

29 Life in a Bubble

I've seen the future, and it scares the daylights out of me.

While traveling with a good friend recently, I stayed overnight with an old friend of his. The next morning, blinking sleepily at each other over cold cereal and coffee, my friend and I wondered out loud about the day's weather.

Our host instantly disappeared, returning moments later with a complete forecast.

"Going to be sunny," he informed us. "High in the lower 70s."

We were packing our belongings, getting ready to head out, when another question arose.

"What's it like outside now?" asked my friend, debating between an old, wrinkled, long-sleeved or an old, wrinkled, short-sleeved shirt.

Our host slipped past me, heading away from the outside door and up the staircase.

"Where are you going?" I asked.

"Upstairs to my computer," he said.

"Why?"

"To see what the temperature is outside."

I indicated the front door, inches away from where he stood minutes before.

"How about we just open this door and go outside and see for ourselves?" I asked.

Sometimes the obvious is too simple. We all laughed at how technologically dependent we've become. But as we packed and left town, I began to find the subject less laughable and more frightening.

Thinking back on how we'd gotten to that point in our trip, I realized we'd literally used computers every step of the way.

My friend first sent me an e-mail proposing the trip. When I agreed and proposed a side trip, I did it via the same method. When we mapped out our trips, we didn't reach for a folded paper map. We each went to a popular Internet mapping service and plugged in the coordinates for the trip. Considering our trip took him 400 miles north of his home and me 300 miles west of mine, the only way we could contact each other would be our other small computers, our cell phones. How did I find his phone number when I needed to reach him? Why, it was stored in my trusty PDA – "Personal Digital Assistant" – of course.

The longer our trip went on, the more it became clear to me I'm living in a bubble of technology. My world is slowly becoming limited to what information I can retrieve, input, share and call up by computer. Long on information, short on interaction.

Then the unthinkable happened. As the day wore on, I noticed the little bars indicating the battery strength on my cell phone steadily declining. Looking through my gear for the car charger, a sudden realization washed over me: I could be hundreds of miles from home with a dead cell phone.

Fear took over. We were camping in a tent that night. Nowhere to plug in my computer, no way to send e-mail or get directions. Panic set in. I began to plan what would be my final call before it went totally dead. I'd call my wife, tell her to tell the kids I love them, only to discover an annoying beep interrupting our conversation.

Then, just as I closed my now-dead cell phone, I spotted an electronics store in a small town and turned in. Minutes later I walked out with a car charger for my cell phone — and comfortably settled back into my bubble. ●

30 Is Being a Hypocrite Key to Parenting?

"It happened right here," I said to my 14-year-old son, our car cresting the hill along a winding two-lane road. "A friend of mine crossed the center line driving drunk and killed a 16-year old girl."

"Whoa," he said, "really?"

"Yeah," I said, thinking back to the day my friend pointed out the spot on the road to us a few weeks after the fatal accident. "And he lives with it every day of his life."

A heavy silence accompanied my son and me as we continued down the long hill.

Not the most pleasant of conversations, but one of many I feel strongly my son needs to have with me.

I'm learning being a hypocrite is a critical part of being a parent, in some ways.

As adults, we all remember the incredible feeling of immortality from our early youth. Our minds and hearts are fighting for control — all under the incredibly destabilizing influence of awakening hormones. Granted, we've tried to live our lives as well as possible. Yet there are things in our pasts we'd just as soon not be on public display or scrutiny, particularly as our children grow into young adults.

But, for the sake of our children, we find ourselves preaching a "do as I say" rather than "do as I do."

Parenting, to a great extent, is about expectations. Explaining them is easy; managing them in the heat of battle is something completely different. Growing up, the one thing I never wanted to do was disappoint my parents. Our home was not full of rules. Instead, there were expectations. Forget peer pressure. The bond of respect — even as a teen — I never wanted to jeopardize. That's not to say I was perfect. I wasn't. I'm not sure anyone is, or will ever be. But there are stories I feel strongly about sharing with him in hopes maybe they will stay with him in those powerful moments of youth and maybe — just maybe — be there for him.

Yes, he knows about another good friend of mine, the top player on our high school golf team who was getting ready to report to college on a full ride, only to be killed in an single-car accident involving alcohol. And the many kids I knew with top SAT test scores who thought they could walk the line between drugs and school. A good many, as I've told him, thought wrong — losing their dreams and futures. A couple of them even lost their lives.

As my son and I continued down the road that day, we talked about how the driver who killed the 16-year-old girl must have felt — and feels to this day.

The line between preaching and teaching is fine and easy to misjudge. It is my hope that by being open and honest about my experiences, I can help him create expectations to last him a lifetime. ●

31 The Last Thunderstorm

One day, without fanfare, I'll hear my last thunderstorm.

Nothing reminds me more of my place in life than those brief moments after a crashing clap of thunder - and the residual sound of feet racing down the hallway.

"You know," my wife said to our daughter once, "what's going to happen when you move out and get married?"

"Guess I'll just have to live next door," she said.

As a child, I thought thunderstorms were a mystery of nature, a powerful exhibition no one – let alone me – could control. Decades later, I still remember the confusion when a storm woke me in the night, greeting me with a strange and powerful aversion to being alone. But one day, without any notice, the feeling evaporated and left me alone in my room with flashes of light painting the walls of my bedroom.

I know how my parents might've felt the night of the last thunderstorm, a night when being alone was more traumatic for them than for me.

This strange feeling lay dormant for many years, until my wife and I brought children into the world. As a parent my mind began a new course of thought whenever a thunderstorm approached. No longer did I think about how the yard needed rain or wonder whether the car windows were rolled up. Instead,

I began to count the moments until I heard footsteps coming down the hallway and felt a small body jumping into our bed to share our pillows.

As a parent, you learn your job is not always just teaching your son to keep his elbow up while batting or letting go of the bicycle seat as your daughter wobbles forward on two wheels for the first time. Parenting contains a lot of time for just being there. No special words of wisdom to impart, no great secrets of life to share. Just be. And thunderstorms, I now recognize, are one of those wonderful moments in life that remind us of our special place as a parent. No reasoning about how thunder is created by changes in weather patterns is necessary. When lightning blazes silhouettes against the walls and thunder shakes the room, science is a poor substitute for the knowledge that you're not alone in the world.

One day every parent will hear the last thunderstorm. That night, lightning will flash weirdly at the windows, waves of thunder will shake the walls -- and nothing else will happen. No feet will race down the hall, no one will need to share your pillow in the middle of the night. A strange feeling will reawaken as you find yourself alone when the final clap of thunder rolls off into the distance. ●

32 Memories, the Drink of Life

"You realize," said a friend to me earlier this week, "you've less time ahead of you with your daughter living under your roof than behind you."

It wasn't the first time that mathematical equation had crossed my mind. The emotions of my friend's words, however, gripped me with an unexpected power. You see, with my daughter turning 10 years old this week, both my children have crossed into double-digits, leaving me with only memories of parenting small children.

It's funny how time begins to accelerate at a pace we could never imagine as the years and memories accumulate behind us. Diapers and nightly feedings are forever - or so they seem. Suddenly and without any warning, that stage is behind you and you're swimming in a brand new sea of alphabet soup, relentlessly sung at by a gigantic purple dinosaur.

There are very few words more honest than "enjoy your children while they're little because it'll be over before you know it."

The stage of life in which I am the omniscient holder of the secrets of life is quickly - and quietly - coming to an end. Today, the phrase "my little girl" remains a part of my basic vocabulary even though my eyes reveal a much different picture. I now realize the phrase is probably more for my peace of mind than for accuracy. In her room, butterflies are now giving way to photographs of her favorite musical groups with names I can barely pronounce who perform not a single song I can identify.

Yes, with her brother now 14, I've now crossed into a world of double-digits and I feel as if I'm starting over. Just when I thought I could look up from the steering wheel and enjoy the scenery, the road abruptly changed - and I have to learn how to drive again.

Parenting, I'm learning, is about starting over again. And again. And again. Children grow up. Outside influences leak in, altering the center of gravity in the relationships with our children. The rules we followed last week suddenly become outdated, and sometimes irrelevant, in the face of changes. As children grow up, they learn the healthy habit of questioning and challenging the world around them. As their parents, become the teething ring for a sharpening mind.

A decade of raising children has been the single most rewarding and beautiful experience in my life. There is no greater blessing from God than to be entrusted with the responsibility of caring for and guiding children through life. But like all things, this chapter too will end.

Yes, my friend is right. Mathematically, I've probably fewer years ahead of me than behind me with my daughter living under my roof. But as someone told me recently, "memories are the drink of life." And although I'm beginning to feel the first twitches of thirst I've still plenty of water to collect from the well of life. ●

33 Is Anyone Home?

Did anyone notice cell phones, e-mail, voice mail — all designed to help us stay connected — make it harder than ever to speak to a human being?

My frustration came to a head during a meeting, as a friend lamented that he'd left messages on several different phones for someone to call him back with guidance on a critical project.

"I'm beginning to wonder," he said, "if anyone is ever home anymore."

Afterwards, I found myself much more aware of how the so-called technology boost is impacting my day-to-day actions. Back at the office, I had four voice mails and eight e-mails. Returning the calls, I left three voice mails and one message with an assistant (how retro) and responded to each e-mail. Later, I made a phone call to another office and left yet another a voice mail.

Toward the end of the day, something unusual happened during another call. After a voice identified itself on the other end of the line, I was greeted with silence.

"Hello?" I said, as confident as if I were walking though a dark room full of furniture.

"Hello?" came the reply — not an echo.

Stumbling — hitting my big toe on an oversized sofa I

could not see — I tried to save face.

"Roger?" I said with hesitation.

"Yes, right here."

I was out of my element. Where was the 10-second message asking me to leave a time, date and number? There I was, talking with a live human being, without a plan.

After that false start, I regained my composure and began my conversation, the one I'd intended to complete at a later time when Roger retrieved his voice mail.

We can't seem to go anywhere today without our devices -- the current buzzword for cell phones, live PDAs, etc. They exert a strange power over us, tricking us into believing we can be in better control of our lives if we use them.

Five of us attended that earlier meeting. Two were interrupted by cell phones or their BlackBerrys, and we had to wait while the device was satisfied. Doesn't take long to figure out who's in control in this scenario, does it?

Technology is our friend, we are led to believe. Marketers tell us we are indispensable and irreplaceable and that we need to be connected 24/7. With satellites circling the globe and cell towers popping up like dandelions in spring, you'd think we'd never be out of touch. So why isn't anyone ever at home? ●

34 Backpack Carries Weight of the World

Without a hint of immediacy in his step, the bearded man meandered across the busy city street. Light drizzle showered around him, but each footstep matched the heavy pace of the one before.

He carried a gray, oversized backpack across his shoulders. But as my windshield wipers cleared away the mist, I could see in his eyes that the burden on his shoulders didn't just come from the pack, but also from the weight of the world.

Homelessness is not an easy subject for most of us to stomach. It is a dirty, unnamed blemish on our community. And to many of us, it is a daily opportunity to reflect on our personal blessings, yet rarely do we recognize it as such.

If you've continued to read this column to this point, thank you. This is not the most comfortable of subjects to acknowledge, or to think about. I'll admit it is not something I reflect on regularly.

But for me, this bearded man — the one with the weight of the world on his shoulders — did not disappear after his silhouette melted into the mist of my rearview mirror that morning.

I don't pretend to know the answers to the world's questions. Furthermore, I understand people often are where they are in life because they are the sum of their decisions. Life can be cruel. A couple of poor decisions can wreck a life. But does that mean I should let people with wrecked lives be erased from my consciousness in the blink of an eye — the little time it takes for me to turn the corner at the end of the block?

I could simply say I don't know this man. But is that the truth? Is it unreasonable to think he feels cold, pain, happiness or sadness? If so, then I've more in common than I've ever cared to admit to myself. Somewhere there is a mother and father — and possibly a family -- attached to this man and his gray backpack.

Homelessness is not a recent phenomenon, and it can't be eradicated by throwing money at the problem. People may be more likely to open their hearts to a stray kitten or dog than to another human being. We instinctively turn away from pain, perhaps hoping that in doing so the problem will resolve itself. Unfortunately, that is not so — particularly in this case. Each of our homeless is an individual with his own set of problems.

We all have turning points in our lives, and I guess this man with the heavy footsteps is mine. I'll never forget wondering to myself, "Why isn't this guy with the heavy backpack rushing to get across the street, with all this traffic?" But then I could see something completely different weighing on his shoulders. And at that moment, I finally understood. ●

35 Bigfoot Discovered at Home

Carefully examining the outline of the footprints, I quickly realized I was seriously outsized by visitors to our home. Simple deduction revealed the visitors had a distinct advantage in both height and bulk over me.

I called my wife over to the pile of shoes deposited by our front door last weekend as the group of teenage boys rumbled around upstairs. When I compared my foot to several different pairs of shoes our son's friends had left behind, it was clear that I, though the senior male in the house, was no longer the biggest kid on the block. The colorful basketball and hiking shoes assembled near the door dwarfed my feet. As a matter of fact, I probably could have placed my foot — shoe and all — inside most of the boys' shoes.

And so goes life with growing teenage boys and a dad's diminishing role as the Alpha Male.

Later, bearing an offering of four pepperoni pizzas, I knocked on the door of my son's room to find the shoe owners all huddled around a computer in the far corner.

"Hey guys," I said, "Pizzas are here."

Turning away from the screen, they stood up, nearly grazing their heads on the slanted ceiling. Their voices sounded as though they had been routed through a powerful sub-woofer.

I was seriously outmanned -- yes, manned – but I was still top dog. At least, in my mind.

It is a strange feeling the first time you recognize the only advantage you have over a group of kids is the respect of authority.

Don't get me wrong. This is a great group of guys. I've known most of them for years. Only now, something is drastically different. Inside, they are still the same fine young men, but on the outside, they are bigger than my wife and me combined.

I guess I never really thought much about it growing up, the day my parents began to recognize these feelings. One year my friend and I were content camping in the back yard in an old tent, flashlights left on all night to keep us company, and the next year all we could talk about was cars.

A friend's son was my son's age when I last saw him, several years ago. Equally well-mannered, polite and smart. Her son now towers well above six feet and has crossed the 200-pound mark of muscle and bone.

I know the metamorphosis of my child into a young adult would be significant and emotional to me as a parent. What I didn't expect was that it would arrive so quickly.

You'd think at some point I'd get used to all these changes, right? Yet last weekend, with all those giant feet making themselves at home in my son's room, I once again found myself in uncharted territory. ●

36 Calendar a Poor Measure of Time

How, I wondered long ago, can you be married — or together — so long you can't remember how many years have passed?

As my wife and I approach yet another anniversary, I'm beginning to understand how marriage is not measured by calendar years, but by the stages of life a couple experiences together. A calendar, I'm finding, is a poor record of events that operate without a clock.

Listening carefully to friends around me, I'm learning we can probably break life down into a handful of significant events: becoming newlyweds, new parents of small children, parents of teenagers and finally, parents of college students.

"You remember that stage?" I inquired of my wife recently, watching a young couple wrestling with an overloaded diaper bag, stroller and department store door. Even without benefit of x-ray vision, most parents can guess the bag's contents: fresh diapers and wipes, snacks and bottles, clean clothes and burp cloths and bibs. I carry less for overnight business trips.

The new parent stage arrives with a bang, seamlessly blending into the parents of young children stage — a time when you can finally leave them in a room by themselves for a moment without guilty thoughts of what could happen. This stage is commonly identified with non-spill cups and -- for us -- a large purple dinosaur dancing around on television. You find yourself the primary teacher of everything to a young, eager mind with the absorption properties of a giant sponge. It is among the most satisfying of parenting stages.

Then come the teenage years. Granted, my wife and I are just entering this period, but we are finding the teens offer a completely different perspective for both parent and child. Among the most unexpected revelations in this stage is how interesting we find our 14-year-old son. His views of the world, his questions about life and the directions in which his curiosity leads him amaze us. Teenagers seem to be in a constant cycle of personal reinvention. But this stage also is humbling for parents like me, who find their intellect pushed to its limit as their children's questions become more complex and challenging each day.

For the next stage, college age, I'm relying on the honest words of my friends. For some of them, the college years have been a difficult and emotional transition to make as parents. It is a stage where the ambient level of noise in their houses goes down. No longer is a subwoofer thumping from a bedroom upstairs. When the phone rings, callers actually want the homeowners – a major shakeup for parents after so many years of child-monopolized phone lines.

Still, I laughed as my wife repeated a conversation she had with a friend. Their last child had just moved off to college, leaving him and his wife alone at home for the first time in years.

"That must be quite an adjustment," my wife said to him.

"Yes," he said with a grin. "But nothing like when they first arrived on the scene."

And so another anniversary approaches and my wife and I look at each other and smile, understanding -- at this stage -- that our actual number of married years is irrelevant. It is the experiences we share that are most important in bigger picture of our lives together. ●

37 Package Contains Hidden Meaning

Her hands trembling, the woman struggled mightily with the simple task of closing the lid of a cardboard box. A long line of people, seemingly unaware of the woman's challenge, stretched the length of the local post office.

"May I help you?" I asked, stepping out of my place in line.

Graciously, she accepted my offer.

The box contained an oversized teddy bear, a gift for her father. While she worked to manipulate the fluffy form, to make it fit beneath the lid, she shared with me her struggles with Parkinson's disease.

"Been on full-time disability for several years now," she explained.

She reached for a rolling tape dispenser to seal the box, the bear – at last securely packed for his journey -- beneath its lid. I returned to my place in line and she to hers. As the line of customers thinned, we struck up another conversation. Not about her quest to close the box this time, but about her gift.

"It's a Build-a-Bear," she said, sharing how she had hidden a special voice message for her father inside the stuffed fellow. "You can completely customize these. This one is made especially for him."

What struck me most about this chance encounter was this woman's total focus. It was all about the task and not at all about the challenges. Her concern was for the person at the delivery address. Battling a difficult and debilitating disease, this woman chooses to focus on what she still is able to do for others, not on what she can no longer do for herself.

I thought about the courage fueling journey of that bear. That perfect green hat, selected and secured onto tiny ears. Puffy paws threaded through small openings in a just-right custom vest. Simple tasks – that is, if you don't have Parkinson's disease.

When it was my turn to approach the mail clerk, I was hyper-sensitive to each easy motion I made as I handed him my envelope. Reaching for my billfold was effortless. Flipping it open and grabbing a couple of dollar bills would not present any difficulty – that was a given. I noticed a pen, wondered how different my signature would look, thought about how even placing a stamp in its proper place on an envelope would be a challenge without the guidance of a steady hand.

Finishing my business, I turned to leave and caught sight of my new hero working with another clerk, her father's gift on the counter next to her. From that moment forward, I have carried another gift, one she unknowingly shared with me: I no longer take for granted that closing a cardboard box is a simple task for so many of the people who walk the streets with me every day.●

38 Living with Eyes Wide Open

"Did you ever notice," my daughter said as we rode bikes around the neighborhood the other night, "that clouds seem to go on forever?"

At the tender age of 10, my daughter is not about to let me go numb to the world around me.

"What do you mean?" I asked.

Slowing down her bike, she pointed out how the clouds above us move across the sky. Dark, heavy clouds moved quickly below the large, lumbering white clouds at higher elevations.

As we continued along the road, I began to consider how easy it is for me to take big bites of information while losing sight of the exquisite details of life's fabric, squashing my ability to appreciate a unique moment.

In the clouds above, I began to notice – thanks to my daughter's observation -- much more detail than in my simple one-dimensional impression of the sky. I saw clouds temporarily blocking the sun, diffusing bright sunlight. Just as she said, clouds did indeed cross the sky forever, reaching the ground far in the distance. Contrasting colors in the white pillow-clouds and the dark, racing clouds suddenly fascinated me.

Growing up is not always a positive experience. As adults, we find ourselves working to take in more and more information, often at the expense of the little details that make life so special in the first place. Speed reading teaches us to digest information in groups of words, not allowing for the luxury of immersing ourselves in the writing. It renders us unable to revel in the beauty of the clever play of words so painstakingly drafted by the author.

Living at the speed of life means living too fast to fully appreciate the fullness of the moment.

Can you name three discoveries you made on your own in the past year, without coaching or recommendation? A bottle of wine you've never before tasted, purchased on the spur of the moment? A musician whose work you explored simply because the liner notes piqued your interest? A tiny restaurant hiding between buildings in a less-traveled section of town? Such discoveries can be made, but not at the speed of life.

Seeing the clouds from my daughter's perspective reminded me of a very important principle: Living with your eyes wide open is easier said than done. To fully appreciate the beauty of life, we must slow down and recognize that all clouds are not alike -- and that the sky does indeed go on forever. ●

39 Arizona Sunset Reveals Secrets

Ambling across the hotel parking lot, an elderly couple paused to enjoy sunset as the Arizona desert sky, blazing red and pink hues against a mountain skyline, darkened for the night.

Watching nature's breathtaking show from a westward-facing wooden bench, my wife and I observed the couple as they turned our way. The man's blue suspenders sculpting his round torso, his wife dressed neatly in a pantsuit and gleaming white tennis shoes, they settled on an adjacent bench.

We all sat in silence as the final fingers of light slipped below the horizon.

"Sure is a beautiful sunset tonight," I said.

Snuggled against her husband, the woman smiled and patted his arm. I noticed his stern demeanor soften at her touch, and we began an exchange about the circumstances that brought us together, on these wooden benches, to watch this particular sunset.

"Our granddaughter is getting married tomorrow," the wife shared, her eyes beaming with pride. His part of the comment was limited to "humph" and a slow nod of agreement. Casual exchanges about children, hometowns and marriage revealed a startling fact.

"Fifty years we've been married now," she said, he again

briefly lifting his chin off his plaid, short-sleeved shirt by way of acquiescence.

"Wow." I said. "Fifty years is a remarkable accomplishment. Surely you've some advice you can pass along to us?"

Again the husband lifted his chin as she said, "Well, I'd say we know how to argue."

My confusion must have been evident as I searched for an appropriate reply.

"We each know when to start," she clarified, "and when to stop."

Turning her head to look up into her husband's eyes, she reached over to touch his forearm. Staying true to his pattern of semi-silent acknowledgment, he this time turned and smiled sheepishly.

Moments later, darkness settled in to close the conversation. We said our goodnights and went to dinner. But the words of this 50-year veteran of marriage continued to resonate inside my head – and heart.

She spoke about arguing out of conflict, but her words said even more about respect for your marriage — and for the other person in your marriage. It is important to say your piece but also to understand personal attacks are out of bounds.

I admired her for being able to sum up the success of their enduring relationship in a single sentence. No recommendation for a self-help book from the bestseller list. No need for a long-winded dissertation on the do's and don't's of relationship-building. Just a single, common-sense concept: Respect your partner.

And as the days accumulate, the clarity and honesty of that marriage prescription from the woman in gleaming white tennis shoes will remain with me. ●

40 Old Family Home, Like Values, Remains

"Excuse me, do you know where this little cottage is?"

Unsteady footage from a hand-held video camera shows an older woman standing before a weather-worn stone building. My cousin's voice, coming from behind the camera, is polite and respectful as he approaches the woman for directions.

I am watching the documentation of his 5,000-mile pilgrimage, a journey from his San Francisco home to the Scottish Highlands. On film, he searches for the small cottage where our mothers – sisters – spent their childhood. His only guide is a well-worn, sepia-toned postcard exchanged decades ago between the sisters. My mother wrote of a childhood memory on the card, of naughty little girls whose switch-brandishing mother chased them along the banks of a nearby stream. My cousin has carried the postcard across the Atlantic Ocean, hoping it will further his quest to find a tiny village where less than 70 people resided, including our mothers.

In heavy highland brogue, the woman begins to speak. On film, her words roll along in a combination of sounds rarely heard on this side of the Atlantic. Her language sounds like some distant, melodic relative of the English language to those unfamiliar with the dialect. She carefully studies my cousin's postcard, printed in the 1930s, and its depiction of four little girls strolling past four-room streamside cottage. She points back toward the road and he retraces his steps, then starts off in a different direction.

Thomas Wolfe said "You can never go home again." Most of us would probably like to trace the steps of our families, though, just to better understand who we are. We know where we've been and where we are today, but the question of where we came from requires looking a little further back. Who we are - and what we believe - can be heavily influenced by those who came before us.

That is my cousin's purpose. Back in Scotland, his camera turns way from the woman. For a few moments, his footsteps crunching on the gravel pathway are the only sound, and then a tiny cottage near the brook comes into view. A green sedan is parked in front of the now-white cottage, and despite a room addition, window boxes and a picket fence separating living space from the narrow road, the house is clearly recognizable as the one in the postcard. Its identity revealed, the house leaves the screen as the camera turns toward a hand-built stone bridge across a shallow stream. We are home. Here is the place of our mothers' memories, here in the shadows of the rolling highland hills. Here is where they lived the stories they told us when we were children. Here are the village streets the sisters ran though, here the very waters into which they threw stones as young girls.

Suddenly, I see the past with a newfound clarity and depth. I never doubted they were true, but my mother's childhood tales become somehow more authentic to me as I watch my cousin's trek unfold on my screen.

Rarely does a day go by when I don't find myself living by or drawing upon the principles, lessons and values instilled in me by my parents. Room addition, window boxes and white picket fence aside, I have seen the place where those characteristics took root so long ago – and I know now where I come from. ●

41 Life Too Short for Reruns

"Well, there's an hour and a half I'll never get back," my friend had said, rising from his theater seat as the movie credits began to roll.

His comment came to mind during a conversation with another friend, who vowed never again to force herself to finish a lousy book. If she wasn't hooked after the first 100 pages, she said, she'd simply close the book, set it aside and start another.

"Life is too short to waste reading a book if I don't care about the characters," she said.

Isn't it strange how time seemed infinite when we were children, yet as we age we talk about time we'll never get back and life being short? How is it that weekends seem to become shorter with each passing year? And didn't it seem our children were 4 years old for a long time, yet now they seem to be racing through their teenage years, barreling toward adulthood? I feel as if I can literally see time expire — and I'm not willing to waste any of it. Bad movies, television reruns, poorly written books, and all other time-stealers are now my sworn enemies.

Fortunately, a full life is not measured by time alone — nor should it be. A full life is one of unique and powerful experiences. Rewards in life come many times from simply being there for someone else, even if it means doing nothing more than sitting quietly next to them while they cry.

A calendar can be broken down in different ways. Twelve months, 52 weeks, 365 days. How many years before you can legally drive, how many months before your youngest child hits a double-digit birthday, how many shopping days until Christmas. If you actually take the time to figure out the amount of free time you own, the number is alarming.

The average American earns two weeks of vacation per year and is off work two days per week. This adds up to 118 free days per year. And we all know how "free" we are as we race to attend soccer games, visit with relatives, mow the lawn or even sit down to pay the bills on those days. Add to that the statistics showing 26 percent of Americans did not get any vacation time last year, and it's no wonder we feel as if we find ourselves bewildered by how fast the time goes.

Crucial to living a full life is taking the time to seize opportunities hidden throughout our packed days. It is not easy to do, especially when all we'd really like to do on a Saturday afternoon is take a long nap. (Really, napping is not such a bad idea. We need to invest in ourselves, too.) If the measure of a full life is our ability to really live — not just exist -- then making that distinction can mean a world of difference in our daily lives. ●

42 Reach Out and Touch Someone

"Never miss an opportunity to reach out and touch someone's life."

This phrase was uttered by a good friend in response to the question of why he carefully scanned obituaries, births and engagements in the newspaper. It resonates more with me each passing year.

"You never know if a friend's family member could be listed," my friend said. "It gives you an opportunity to demonstrate how you genuinely care about them."

I decided it must be exhausting to put forth that kind of effort, continuously reaching out to people each day -- until I followed his advice one day. That day, I learned for myself what my friend hadn't shared with me: The powerful reward his practice pays to all those involved, including the one reaching out.

Medical experts claim it takes more muscles to frown than to smile, just as the practice of reaching out reaps much more reward than one would expect from simply sending a quick note to someone whose engagement announcement just appeared in the Sunday newspaper. I'm not sure when I first put my friend's advice into action, but I am sure that it makes a positive difference in people's lives.

We're not talking about rocket science here, just un-learning a lifelong practice of standing back and keeping our emotions completely in check. The people in our lives matter, and we do a poor job of letting them know what they mean to us. We should never withhold genuine gestures of appreciation or recognition, but....we do.

In the end, empty flattery does more damage than good for the sender. Face it, we can spot fake sincerity a mile away. But if you can fully follow the spirit of my friend's advice, you soon will appreciate its true value. See, most of us are hardwired to step back, to not "get all up in someone's business." But the truth is that not one of us would send back a card or end a telephone call congratulating, sympathizing with or encouraging us during a significant event in our lives. Very little in the world matters more to us in those times – or at any time -- than to know we are in someone's thoughts.

Yes, my friend's advice requires some investment. It also yields some of the greatest returns you can imagine. We cover ourselves with practiced and protective veneers, but think about the last time you opened an unexpected letter from a friend. Maybe it was one written for no particular reason other than to say hello. Remember how you felt? Beneath that wary exterior, you were deeply touched by the fact that someone had thought about you, had taken the time to jot down a few lines and drop them in the mailbox.

It starts with one day. Today is good. Look for an opportunity, then reach out and touch someone's life. ●

43 Sky is the Limit for Enduring Love

Hurrying between busy gates, I noticed a couple playing cards on a small wooden table inside the airport coffee shop where my wife and I had paused just long enough to grab a cup. As we rushed off again, their infectious and genuine laughter followed us out the door.

We hadn't stayed long, but I saw that his broad shoulders and big frame dwarfed the older woman, who sat across the table dealing cards his way. Her hair was a blend of gray and black, neatly styled. Both were striking, with strong and individual characteristics, but they shared the same beautiful smile. Their laughter was of a sort that comes only with an easy relationship between close friends.

Our encounter left me wondering: Just how and what makes a relationship so special that a simple game of cards becomes the most wonderful experience in the world? As it happened, I would get the chance to find out as we boarded our plane a few minutes later. Settling in as we prepared for takeoff, I heard a vaguely familiar voice.

"You take the window seat," a woman said, approaching the row in front of us. It was the salt-and-pepper-haired card player, nodding toward her hulking partner as he followed her toward their seats.

"No Mom," he said, flashing an impish smile in our direction. "I fly all the time. Take the window — really."

She stood her ground ever so briefly, then moved to the window seat. When the broad-shouldered young man excused himself to go to the back of the airplane, she seized the opportunity to peer at us though the small gap separating our seats.

"My son," she proudly announced to us, by way of conversation starter. "He's so good to me."

I asked about her accent, which I had picked up on during the window seat speech.

"I came to this country from Yugoslavia 30 years ago," she said. "My son, he was only 5."

Our flight was headed for Chicago, the place she called home for many years. Her late husband worked in the mills along Lake Michigan.

"We had more than 70 relatives in this country when we came over," she said. "We settled on the south side."

Just as she was saying that her son, now 38, is the light of her life, he returned to his seat and it was her turn to excuse herself. He picked up the conversation.

"My mom," he said with pride. He had no way of knowing his opening words were nearly identical to hers.

"This trip is a Mother's Day present," he said. "Her mom isn't doing too well and is in her 90s. Mom doesn't like to fly alone and I'm going that way for a business meeting. A great opportunity — kind of killing two birds with one stone."

His tone indicated the trip was not one of burden, but of love and respect. We talk on as other passengers wrestle with luggage and overhead bins.

"I moved down to Florida about 10 years ago and she lives down here, too," he said as his mother returned. She again prodded him to take the window seat as the plane prepared to leave the gate.

Soon after the plane reaches cruising altitude, I hear a familiar sound from their row. Through the seat gaps, I can see mother and son once again laughing over a game of cards. My question has been answered: It is love that makes their game of cards such a wonderful experience, the same love they've carried for each other for nearly 40 years. ●

44 Parents Need to Look at Sunsets

I feel myself becoming disoriented, shopping with my wife at a clothing store.

"Did we ever buy clothes that small?" I ask her confusedly, indicating a tiny, brightly colored pair of shorts hanging on the rack. The hanger dwarfs the clothing.

My wife smiles at me pityingly, indicating the tag. It reads "6–9M." Somewhere in the dim reaches of my memory I recall shopping for sizes marked with the letter M, but it seems like a lifetime ago. I can't remember what it means. And these shorts look more like they would fit one of our 10-year-old daughter's discarded dolls than a human child.

Looking around the store, where for years we've shopped for our daughter's clothing, I suddenly understand the significance of the baby strollers populating the center checkout aisle. My wife and I leave the store with the mutual, painful realization that our days of shopping there have come to an end.

I guess another stage is behind us.

I'm recognizing the need to fight my tendency toward letting life operate on autopilot, the need to stop carelessly letting moments slip away with little notice. Life moves forward every day without pause, leaving to us the personal responsibility of acknowledging the changes around us.

This hit home again last week while I was poking through a little used chest of drawers in the basement. Just below a layer of odd papers in the top drawer, I find a 3x5 color photograph of a 4-year-old boy chasing a soccer ball. His uniform, obscured by the bright yellow practice jersey, hangs to his knees. A rush of memories floods my mind — our son's first year of soccer. I recall how, at that age, a child making physical contact of any kind with the ball is a major success. An entire decade separates the little boy in the photograph and the computer-obsessed teenager in the upstairs bedroom who will take the field this fall for his high school team.

I continue to stare at the photograph in my hand. I not only remember placing it in the clear plastic frame, but also displaying it on my desk at work. I struggle to identify the year and location of the photograph. Disorientation again takes over, until some sharp noise upstairs snaps me back to the present.

Don't get me wrong — I love life. I believe we all should embrace every sunrise and the amazing, unknown possibilities it brings. What I'm realizing, though — particularly as a parent — is that it is a great mistake only to look forward and never back over my shoulder, to not also enjoy the sunset and the memories it represents. ●

45 Love Turns Hogs into Yogurt

Until I met Ray, I didn't think buying hogs and selling yogurt could have too much in common.

"Heck, son, they tell me I've bought and sold over $3 million in hogs over the years," says the 78-year-old, twice-retired man as he leans on the green wrought iron railing next to me, a cold beer in his hand. Sweat beads form on his forehead in the early afternoon Georgia heat, and deep wrinkles spread outward from his blue eyes like rays of sun.

"Yep, I've just retired again," he says. "Sold my chain of yogurt shops to my daughter and son-in-law. Me and the wife took this trip as a getaway of sorts."

He motions to a woman in a floral dress sitting near the pool below us.

"She's a good girl," he says. "Second wife. Lost my first wife a few years back to cancer."

Life throws curveballs, Ray adjusts. His positive outlook is infectious. But I notice his accent doesn't match up with Southern Georgia, so I ask him about it. His answer makes me smile.

"Indiana," he says. "Valparaiso." The next exit down the interstate from my hometown, I tell him.

"Are you kiddin' me?" he says, shaking his head in disbelief. The creases around his eyes deepen as he laughs from his toes.

He asks questions about the area, it being decades since he's "been home." I'm not much help, as the landmarks he mentions are long gone, replaced by mammoth retail box stores and abandoned storefronts.

Our conversation returns to hogs and yogurt.

"Traveled all around," he says. "Moved, too. Spent a good while down here in southern Georgia before the company called me and my first wife back up north."

He pauses, taking a long drink from the glass bottle. He chuckles, then continues his story.

"We moved in January," he says. "Snowed like heck. Cold as…well, you get the picture. About a month after we get settled I get a call from my wife saying the house in Georgia hasn't sold yet and she's going back. Tells me I can keep the snow — she's out of there."

His wife settled back into their old home, and Ray was trying to make things work long distance when she phoned him.

"One day she calls and tells me she's taken a part-time job at a local yogurt shop, just to stay busy," he says. "The owners are calling it quits. She wants me to buy the business. I think to myself, what the heck do I know about yogurt? Heck, I didn't even like it."

But Ray loved his wife, so he retired from the hog business, leaving behind his friends, his reputation, and his calling in life — for yogurt, a food he didn't even like.

He tells me when he got to Georgia, he couldn't sit still — even in his retirement, running a yogurt store. He ended up opening a half-dozen shops in Florida and Georgia over a few short years. He loves the buzz of business, the chase. Life, Ray says, is to be lived on the field, not viewed from the sidelines. His feet and body are in constant motion. I wonder how he sleeps, with that much energy and enthusiasm pouring out.

Ray's wife closes her book, gets to her feet and starts up the ornate wrought iron staircase where we're standing. Ray introduces her to me as easily as if he and I were long lost neighbors, then reaches out and shakes my hand. His palm is hard, his fingers strong, his smile warm. He turns to open the door for his wife, and we part.

And I remain inspired by the man who loved his wife so much he turned hogs into yogurt. ●

46 Youngest is Not Always Young

When is a 10-year-old not 10 years old? When she's your youngest child.

My wife and I sat in our favorite overstuffed chair together earlier this week, struggling with the realization that our youngest child is no longer all that young.

Watching our son go off to kindergarten a decade ago did not hit us nearly as hard as watching his sister four years later. To this day, I can remember how completely empty the house felt for a few hours each morning. Ask any parent. The day your youngest goes off to school for the first time is a day you realize you're passing a significant milestone. The youngest is always your baby. Parents seem to revel in helping their oldest children reach for the next rung on the maturity ladder, but we have mixed feelings when our youngest attempt to do the same.

With a first child we seem eager to mark their progress, quietly rooting in the background as they gain their footing in a more mature environment. We all remember when they learned to ride bikes without training wheels or took their first wobbly steps across the kitchen floor. But somehow we don't have the same passion for progress with our youngest. Maybe we're just hoping we can fool the calendar.

Our son, now 14 is eyeing his learner's permit, and I'm more accepting of his progress than of my daughter's quest to leave Barbie dolls behind her. Universally, we parents seem to lose our grip on what we are willing to accept as reality with each step our youngest takes forward. It's time to accept that, 14 and 10-year-olds, my wife and I are no longer the parents of two young children.

We can accept the knowledge that each year's back–to–school clothes will be a size larger, but we are strangely surprised when they toss questions our way about why we're sending soldiers to the opposite side of the globe to fight a war.

Nature works against parents in this battle. As the older child matures and begins to spread wings of individuality and independence, it's only natural the younger will start to do the same. It is as if a tractor is steadily pulling the youngest along into maturity. Parents eventually realize there is very little we can do to slow it down.

At least, that's the conclusion my wife and I reached as we sat in our favorite chair together. We know in our hearts our daughter will always be our baby, but we now understand youngest is no longer an accurate reflection of her age – just of her position in our family. ●

47 Dads Lead Through Example

While you weren't looking, Dad, I was.

I thought I'd drop you this note, not just because it is Father's Day, but also because I'm not sure I've ever let you know what an important role you play in my life. You may not realize it, but many of the most important lessons I learned from you didn't come from any formal, sitting-at-the-kitchen-table teaching. Instead, I learned them in those little, seemingly innocuous moments when I silently watched you from the sidelines.

I don't mean the mechanics of cutting the front lawn. I mean how you reacted when the mower wouldn't start. Or the quiet, analytical way you considered your options when television stopped working. I remember how you'd grab your big, mysterious box of vacuum tubes, a funny black box with red and black probes, and then methodically diagnose the problem. To this day, I remember how you demonstrated that the first thing to do when faced with a problem is to think it through.

Your lessons extended beyond teaching me how to repair my overheating car ("always start with replacing the thermostat first — it's the cheapest and nine times out of 10 the problem") or reminding me to slip an empty bread bag over the oil filter when removing it ("it catches the extra oil and reduces the clean-up time"). The really big lessons for me were the work of a completely different set of tools.

I remember the day I drove your brand-new Dodge Aspen over a parking lot curb, splitting the transmission housing wide open. As I stood in the driveway, watching the bright red fluid leak onto the driveway as you crawled beneath the car, you said very little. I nervously babbled about the wet snow in the parking lot, about how I was sure I wasn't driving too fast for conditions -- what teenager doesn't? You squeezed out from under the car, stood up beside me, sighed deeply — and then said the kindest words I never, ever expected to hear: "Well, at least you boys weren't hurt."

Right then and there I learned a lesson I continue to draw upon today in nearly every aspect of my life. You were disappointed that I recklessly damaged your new car -- you got around to that next -- but I knew from then on you valued me more than any material possession in life. And that moment, watching how you deal with that situation, changed me forever.

When Mom died, it crushed all of us. My brother and I were barely into our teens and you had your hands full. But you were there for us. Sure, we all had our difficult days in that testosterone-filled house, but I never doubted how much you loved us, or how deeply you loved and missed Mom. You never complained, never lashed out at the world or invited your teenage sons to play the victim card. Instead, you did your very best to raise us to be honest, hard-working, respectful adults. And for that, I thank you, from the bottom of my heart.

You see, whether you know it or not, I've been watching. Thank you for being there and helping me understand how to be a good person and a good father.

Happy Father's Day, Dad. ●

48 A Case for Holding Hands

When did you last take time to hold hands with the one you love?

I watched through my windshield as an older couple crossed the road in front of me — arms intertwined, hands clasped together. Dressed in a light jacket and felt hat, sporting a neatly trimmed mustache, the man walked proudly attached to a small woman with a colorful scarf pulled across her hair. As they stepped onto the sidewalk they neither parted hands nor broke stride. Holding hands for them clearly was a result of their beautiful state of mind, not physical dependence on the other.

I love to hold hands with my wife for the same reason.

"Do you want to go for a walk?" my wife asked me the other night, adding "It's not nearly as dark as it looks outside," an inside joke we use regardless of the time of day, referencing our penchant for sunset walks.

"Sure," I said, seeing the mid-afternoon sunlight streaming through the living room skylights.

And as we always do, we barely made it off the front porch before we found our hands clasped together, slowly swinging to the rhythm of our walk. It surprises me when people tease us about this habit, something we began as college students nearly 25 years ago. There is electricity in her touch, something I've never felt from anyone else. The coolness of her skin against the warmth of mine, the way her fingers fit effortlessly in mine

-- there is a spark, each and every time. Rarely when we take a walk does my mind not flash back to our early dates, when we first discovered this phenomenon.

But the memories don't stop there. With only a few steps, I can see us walking along the Atlantic shoreline at sunrise last year or even strolling beneath the towering red rocks of Sedona, Arizona. The walks behind us are investments in the heart, but not the type measured on a cardiograph. What that older couple reinforced for me is that there might not be a limit on how long the magical spark of the heart can last, if you take the time to keep the embers burning. ●

49 Peeling Back the Cocoon

Behind the counter of a well-appointed reception area, the haunting questions hung in the air: "You have a daughter, don't you? Don't you just wonder sometimes how we're supposed to raise them in the world today?"

The woman, momentarily allowing the phones beside her go unanswered, is troubled about something. Her dark eyes give away her feelings. But she's not angry with anyone in particular. She's just frustrated at the effect our culture has on young teenage girls. Still, her passionate words strike uncomfortably close to home as I think about my 10-year-old daughter.

Obviously, my interrogator loves her daughter very deeply and is alarmed by the signals our culture sends to children. The clothes, the music and the expectations paint a confusing picture for young girls. That this woman immigrated to America from a much different culture only adds to her frustration. In this land of free speech, she is starting to realize freedom has a price. Unfortunately, for many kids today, freedom comes at the expense of childhood.

Later, looking around my daughter's room, I see evidence of the waves of her concern beginning to wash against my daughter's world. Her favorite music no longer doubles as the theme song for an animated series on television. Hand-colored drawings she created and stuck on a corkboard with a thumbtack are supplanted by photos of movie stars and tattooed rock bands. The erosion of her innocence, I'm afraid, is already under way.

I listened to the woman speak out against the fashions, the culture and the music, and the thought quietly hiding beneath my consciousness began to poke its head up and into my daily thoughts.

"Dad, you're going to have to recognize your little girl is growing up." my daughter retorts when I tease her about her ever-evolving fashion and interests. She's playing with me, and she knows it. What she doesn't yet recognize is how difficult it is for me to accept.

She is our youngest, and when she started kindergarten, it hit me surprisingly hard. Her brother had led the way four years before her, and I was comforted then by the knowledge that she would not start for a few more years. When she did, I watched as her cocoon slowly began to open, letting the world's influences rush in.

Today, I find myself desperately holding onto the peeling pieces of that cocoon as she races to shed them. The harder she works to be older, the more desperate I am to hang on with everything I've got. And so the woman's question still hangs in the air, unanswered. ●

50 Growing Up is Optional

I'm beginning to recognize my own mortality, but not in a manner I ever expected.

"So," asks the nurse, "how did you get this injury to your ribs?"

Looking down at her clipboard she positions her pen to record my answer — only I'm stalling, looking for a graceful way out of telling her the truth. Moments before, I had watched a man in jeans and a white T-shirt approach the front counter with a similar ailment.

"Looks like I lost a wrangle with a ladder," he said.

Waiting for my name to be called in the reception room, I was jealous of his respectable predicament. Thousands of adults climb ladders each year and many "lose a wrangle" with them. No shame. For all I — or the rest of the waiting room knew — he was probably just cleaning his gutters or changing an overhead light on his front porch.

Minutes later, I'm called back to the receiving area where the nurse pre-interviews me for the doctor. Her pen, still motionless, waits for my answer. I tell her where it hurts, dodging the question. But cornered, I am finally forced to give her the answer she needs. The words coming out of my mouth are something I'd expect to hear from my 14-year-old son, not a man who's crossed the threshold of 40.

"I took a fall at the skateboard park."

Her eyes react before her pen. I try to rationalize the situation by telling her I was there with my 10-year-old daughter, hoping maybe she won't think I'm some overgrown kid who refuses to grow up. But the truth is, even my wife that would agree that's a pretty accurate description.

"You know," I told her after returning from the park, "when I'm out there it feels as if I'm 12 years old again. I can't explain it."

I continued, nursing my new injury.

"What I'm beginning to think, though, is I'm not too old to skate, just too old to fall."

Crossing into my 40s is a strange trip. I've skateboarded for more than 30 years, but I'm finally beginning to recognize there may very well be a limit to the things I can learn and do in the future. Especially considering the fact that, on many days, the mere tying of my shoes can be so much work that I've started wearing slip-ons.

Then there is the weight issue. Since when did it take more than cutting back on second portions or adding another mile to the daily run to drop a few pounds? Experts assure me the food is not changing — it's me.

Evaporating inside of me is the bottomless pool of immortality we all draw upon in our youth. I just may need to accept not only my limits but also my mortality.

As for growing up and acting my age, well, that I believe is optional for all of us. And in the words of my daughter: "I didn't sign up for that." ●

51 Surf Shop Reflects Passion for Family

Sometimes it takes a stranger to point out the obvious in life.

"Is this your father?" says the rich, gravelly voice.

I'm standing just inside the door of a small surf shop along the Outer Banks of North Carolina during a family reunion trip. The shop owner, whom I'd met late the night before while visiting his store with my family, greets me at the door as I return, this time with my father in tow. My wife and kids split off, losing themselves in the colorful aisles of tee shirts and surfing merchandise.

"Yes," I answer, turning to introduce my father. "Dad, this is Tony. And this" – gesturing with a wide sweep of my arm – "is Tony's Surf Shop."

Tony is a man of medium build and large personality. His voice is strong, with a hint of an accent foreign to the Carolina coast. His hair is salted with hints of gray, his demeanor that of a man at peace with himself. He passes a cigarette from his right hand and into his left, balancing it with his forefinger against his cup of coffee. Reaching out, he shakes my father's hand with genuine sincerity.

Turning to me, Tony says, "Do you know how lucky you are to have this man in your life every day?"

Tony's love for his own father is evident in the way he

speaks of him.

"I opened up my surf shop 19 years ago," he says. "My father, who brought our family over here 26 years ago from Lebanon, died just before I opened it. I keep a large framed photograph of him in my living room. Every day I walk up to his picture and kiss him. I miss him that much."

My dad is visibly moved by the surf shop owner's heartfelt respect and his passion for the value of family. I look at my watch, knowing we've only about 10 minutes to spend in the shop before we must leave for the airport. I reluctantly say I'd better start corralling the others.

Tony sets down his coffee and cigarette, steps forward and wraps his burly arms around my dad.

"You are so lucky," he again says to me, clamping his broad hands down on my dad's shoulders. "Always value this man. Remember that."

He has no way of knowing a family reunion is responsible for bringing me to this island, to his surf shop. I'm there to reconnect with many family members we see only occasionally, yet somehow this stranger with his strong sense of family instinctively touches the deep pool of emotions behind our trip. The framed photo of his father hanging in his living room is testament to his love of family – and to the sincerity of his words. ●

52 And Then There Were Two

"My youngest starts as a senior in high school this year," said a friend, the look in her eyes matching the catch in her breath as she forces out the words, clearly conflicted.

My time is coming, a time when the home my wife and I keep is radically transformed from the one to which I now return each night. No longer will our evenings be consumed with homework, school sports, and family time. No longer will the dinner table conversation center around what happened at school or which friends the children will visit that weekend.

I know this as surely as I know that when my friend's daughter graduates from high school and moves on to college, only she and her husband will be left at home each night, sitting at the kitchen table for dinner.

I wonder how it will feel the first time my wife sets the table for two? How long will it be until those empty places at the table won't cause our hearts to ache? How long until we can accept that, after nearly two decades of riding the unpredictable waves of parenting, it's back to just the two of us? What a strange and unsettling transition it must be for a couple who've spent the better part of their marriage focused on investing not only their hearts and souls but every spare nickel and dime in the future of their children.

My wife and I are not too different from most people in

our belief that our children are a blessing from God. By entrusting us to not only bring them into the world but to help guide them and prepare them for adulthood, He expects us to be completely sold out, to cherish and nurture them every step of the way. Naturally, their departure must be excruciatingly painful for the ones left clinging to each other at that table set for two.

I returned home from visiting my friend with a renewed focus on my daily life. Looking across the dinner table, I saw our 10-year-old daughter and our son, who enters high school this year, in a completely different light. I know this season is not forever -- I can see the finish line without too much effort. And honestly, that scares me. Each year, we let out a little more of the rope that binds us to our children, allowing them to experience both the successes and setbacks of their choices. Each day, we find ourselves biting our tongues more often, resisting the urge to make their choices for them. Instead, we take on the more difficult role of coaching, standing on the sidelines to offer support as they pick up the pieces or celebrate.

After a lifetime of living for someone else, what happens on that day you go back to setting the table for two? I don't know the answer, but one thing is for sure: I'm glad I won't be alone. ●

53 Living by the Book New for Many

Apparently I'm now a by-the-book kind of guy.

No, I'm not getting rigid to rules as time goes along. I'm referring to computer literacy.

The general population is now broken into two distinct categories of computer users: digital "natives" and digital "immigrants." A friend who shared those labels describes the former as those who were born into a world in which computers always existed, woven into the fabric of their daily lives. The latter, my group, were born before computers ruled the world and must work hard to adapt to our new surroundings.

Methodically plodding through a 700-page manual for the new software program I purchased, I was, according to my friend's definition, working to adapt to my new surroundings.

"Check this out," I said triumphantly to my 14-year-old son as entered the room.

After investing hours of my time reading long chapters on how to manipulate graphics inside the program, I moved the cursor across the screen to show off for my son. He watched over my shoulder as I retraced the steps from the book weighing heavily on my lap. The image did not respond.

I rifled through the manual's pages for help as my son reached around and took the mouse.

"Why don't you just do this?" he said.

Effortlessly, he moved the cursor over to the pull-down menu and selected a function not shown in the pages of my manual. The image instantly reacted. He let go of the mouse and stepped back behind me.

I knew that manual had not left my side since I purchased it the night before, so I had to ask: How did he know to what to do?

"I don't know," he said with a shrug. "Just messing around with the program, I guess."

And so my friend's theory played out before my very eyes, in my own home.

The world is full of those who drive ourselves to adapt to our new surroundings, but hard as we try, we lack something the young natives possess. Best I can figure, it is some combination of intuitiveness and fearlessness.

Never does it enter my son's mind -- or his younger sister's -- to open a book and learn how a computer operates or how to manipulate a new software program. No, the natives of the world just, to use my son's technical term, "mess around" until they get it.

My 10-year-old daughter's computer froze while she was downloading a file. I was in her room, watching, anticipating an "immigrant's" panic — thinking she might ask me for help. Instead, she calmly reached over and pushed the power button, successfully rebooting her computer.

I smiled wryly to myself as I left the room, realizing all the knowledge of all the books will never make me a native in this brave new world. ●

54 Learning New Dance Beautiful

I'm learning to dance without moving my feet at all.

"I'm going to a pool party this weekend," my 10-year-old daughter announced one night at the dinner table.

She shared specifics of location and time, then started leading the daddy-daughter dance that is so natural a part of the relationship between a father and his little girl.

"You know," she said, "it won't be just girls at the pool party."

"You mean boys will be there, too?" I asked.

Tilting her head down and cutting her eyes up at me for extra emphasis, she said, "Yep."

"And I suppose you think you're wearing a two-piece bathing suit?" I said, following her lead.

Her response required no words. She simply raised her dark eyebrows.

"Well, girl, the only two-piece you're wearing to a pool party where there will be boys is a long sweater and blue jeans," I retorted.

Acknowledging my counter-move, she rolled her eyes and grinned at her mother, reveling in knowing what buttons she can push to get a reaction out of me. My wife smiled back, enjoying the innocent taunting as I try to keep up.

The daddy–daughter dance is very special for a father. Foreign to me as I was growing up in a male-only household, I'm quickly learning the steps. The dance is actually based upon a very personal bond. I'm not really sure when I recognized it, but I'm sure I'm not alone in this discovery.

I love both my children with all my heart. To say I love them the same way, however, is to ignore what makes them individuals. As much parents would like to rely on a special code of rules for raising our children, it just doesn't work. Bonds are created between parents and their children — bonds based on mutual trust, confidence and respect. Some areas, our kids recognize, my wife will always be better at dealing with than I am. I can live with that, knowing, over time, it balances out as my areas of expertise emerge.

The daddy-daughter dance is one of those special areas reserved exclusively for me. As much as I love my son, our relationship is painted differently, in a color as unique as he is. Not less or more important — just as different from my relationship with my daughter as the colors seen through a kaleidoscope. Bonds between parents and their children are created through opportunities presented each and every day. We each do our best with that day, that opportunity, that child.

As my daughter literally races toward her teen years, I am learning to appreciate the special moments only she and I can share together. And if those moments are to include me learning a new dance, then I hope I never stop dancing. ●

55 Reverend Preaches by Example

I can still feel the reverend's powerful handshake nearly a decade after he lost his courageous battle with cancer.

His warm hands complemented his gentle personality, and the lesson he embodied - that strength and compassion are not mutually exclusive - continue to inspire me today. If ever a man lived his life with the grace and spirit of the gospels, the reverend did so. A man whose booming voice and solid character easily projected far beyond the modest church chapel in my hometown, his finest sermons came not from the pulpit, but from the manner in which he lived his life as minister, husband and father.

With each passing year, I recognize the hidden seeds of guidance he planted in me as they finally begin to sprout now, years later, when I least expected.

In every stage of my life he was there for me, his large hands and his larger heart. When my mother died unexpectedly, I was barely a teenager. He wrapped his powerful arms around me, helped absorb the absolutely raw pain of loss. A decade later, he joined my wife and me in marriage, his reassuring voice swirling around us like a protective shield. As our family expanded, I could think of no better set of hands to bless our two children before his congregation.

I truly miss this man.

But it is not the actions he performed inside the chapel that

I find coming back to me as an adult. It is how he lived his life every day. I am acutely aware of his example as I find myself approaching the same age he was when cancer entered his life.

Never did the reverend become bitter, even when God was calling him home in the prime of his life, even when he knew he was leaving behind a wife and two young sons. Instead, he led his life to inspire others. Throughout his cancer treatments, he continued to devotedly love his family and minister to his congregation. A long-time believer, his actions spoke even louder than his thundering voice. He trained for and completed a 26.2-mile marathon, raising funds with his feet as they carried his cancerous body along the asphalt route.

Statistically, we all know our lives will cross paths with tens of thousands of individuals. Some will become our intimate friends, while with others we may simply share a smile as we walk by them in lobby of a local bank. What statistics can't tell us is who may be there – if even for a brief instant – to change our lives when we least expect it. ●

56 The American Dream is Alive and Well

With a heavy accent that belied his recent immigration to the United States, the driver welcomed me aboard the long white bus He smiled, greeting the other passengers equally warmly.

Taking a seat in the first row, I noticed a handful of magazines on the seat next to me. Curious, I turned them over to read the titles. A quick glance revealed the driver's pursuit of the American Dream was to consist of a combination of hard work and information gleaned from the well-worn pages of Forbes and Entrepreneur magazines. Flipping through the pages, I learned about dozens of individuals who've blazed the trail the bus driver plans to follow, and I know he has drawn inspiration from them.

Two hours later, we exited a restaurant to find him standing attentively near the bus door. Our group was late returning to his bus, which had been forced to wait for us to finish dinner. Still, he was never anything other than gracious to each and every passenger, and his crisply starched shirt underscored his amazingly professional attitude, his pride in appearance and attention to detail.

So many people are quick to point out why they can't succeed in America, which makes it refreshing to meet immigrants who've come to this nation to chase the American Dream. For them, this is a world of opportunity, a place where dreams come true. Just weeks ago, I flagged down a city cab and met an extremely friendly gentleman who'd arrived in this country a few short years before.

"I can't help but notice your accent," I said, "Where's home?"

With a big smile he turned to me.

"A very little nation – you probably wouldn't recognize it," he said, turning to deftly navigate between other taxies on the busy downtown street. After a pause, he continued.

"Ever hear of Cameroon?"

Our cab making its way beneath the streetlights, he talked about his journey to America and how much he enjoyed driving the cab. He spoke fondly of his home country, but said he'd never go back. America, he said, is a bright shinning light of opportunity.

"I never drove in Cameroon," he added shyly.

We reached my destination, but as we pulled up to the hotel, I was reluctant to end our conversation to end. This hardworking, appreciative, contributing member of society, this man who loved his homeland but was willing to sacrifice everything he knew for better opportunities, now considers America his home.

There are people who will succeed regardless of the obstacles before them. Learning a new language or crossing an expansive, continent-separating ocean will not deter them, and I can't imagine the courage it must take to leave everything and everyone you know behind and move across the globe. But through them, I can see that the American Dream may very well be our nation's greatest legacy. ●

57 Dad's a Testing Ground for Daughters

I have learned to accept that I'm just along for the ride when it comes to my 10-year-old daughter.

"Do you think I could invite a friend over to go trick or treating with me this year?" she asked.

Becoming lost in my own memories of running the neighborhood on Halloween with my friends, I unknowingly place a foot into her clever trap.

"I don't see why not," I said.

While the two of us are watching a movie the next night, learn "a friend" has grown into the plural form.

"Friends?" I ask.

Yes, she said. It will be a couple of other friends come over, too.

She continued to reel me in with her careful manipulation on the third night. She asked how old her brother was when we first let him trick or treat alone, then uses my answer to lobby for even more freedom. My heart sank when I realized it would be the first year we wouldn't tour the neighborhood together.

She let a few more days pass before she plays another card.

"Could I have a friend spend the night after the Halloween

party?" she asks.

I have to think for a minute. Had I missed something here?

"What Halloween party?" I finally say.

"The one we're having here after we trick or treat," she said in a patient, long-suffering tone.

I suddenly understand I've been taken for a very slow, deliberate ride toward her goal of having a party — and I have been oblivious the entire way. Later that night, I confessed to my wife my confusion.

"What's going on here?" I ask, bewildered. "I'm the adult, but she was manipulating me and I didn't even know it."

My wife just laughed at me.

"You just wait," she said. "You've not seen anything yet."

I sat down and paid attention as she warned me about how I'm going to be the primary target as our daughter practices quietly getting her way.

"She already knows it won't work with me," my wife said, "Because I did the very same thing to my dad."

I've come to understand over the last decade that a father and daughter share a very special relationship. What I hadn't realized is how fathers somehow become a danger-free training ground for the little girls we adore. I've begun to unknowingly play a role in empowering her to successfully navigate the outside world.

If playing that role is part of being a good father to my daughter, then count me in. I only hope my wife will be there all the times I am picking myself up and dusting myself off, trying to piece together what just happened to me. ●

58 Camouflage Can't Hide Soldier's Heart

"Where are you headed?" I ask the tall young man standing beside me as our train car jerks away from the airport concourse.

"Home" he says, grinning.

His Marine-issued desert camouflage uniform performs the opposite of its intent when he is surrounded by civilians like me. Sand is inexorably imbedded in the seams and fabric of his tan boots, and a single silver metal identification tag is securely entwined between the laces. Bleached by the sun, his hair is ruggedly cut but neatly kept. Perfect posture amplifies his six-feet-plus height, and his stance projects confidence, strength and pride.

"Just returning from Iraq to visit my family in Pennsylvania for a bit," he adds, answering my unspoken question.

His words remind me that beneath the professional appearance, there is a young man who just wants to go home, plop down on the sofa and watch college football with his family.

A once-black nylon computer case dangles from his shoulder, faded by intense sunlight, grains of sand in every exterior fiber. In a town just west of Baghdad, his unit awaits his return. The name of that town leaves my memory as quickly as it entered, but I know it never will abandon his.

As the train approaches the next platform I turn to him

uncertainly. I want to tell him how much I appreciate what he and his company are doing for the rest of us, but there on that crowded train car, I am surprisingly at a loss for words.

"Thank you," I say. "I really appreciate what you're doing for us over there."

Without a planned speech, I have let my emotions speak for me. He turns and smiles, graciously acknowledging my effort. I look around at our fellow passengers, packed shoulder-to-shoulder, and wonder if they can feel the same strong wave of gratitude for this fine young soldier in our midst. Regardless of our political beliefs, he is doing his duty for all of us, at a sacrifice I could never comprehend.

The train stops and the silver doors slide open. He lifts up his single bag, nods my way, and starts working his way though the crowd. He quickly melts into a rush of people trying to make their holiday flight connections. As the doors close, I discover I am feeling marginalized in light of the heavy burden of responsibility he carries.

I can only pray that one day he and the rest of his company will finally complete their work, safely returning home so they can each stretch out on the sofa to watch a football game with their families. ●

59 Dotted Line Blurs During Holidays

Family is not always determined by blood.

Preserved in the pages of a family Bible, the solid lines of a family tree make it easy to identify blood relatives who gather in our homes during the holidays. But what about the family connected to us by the dotted lines of friendship and fellowship?

As I've gotten older, I've begun to appreciate how blood can be the basis for a holiday gathering, but also that it in no way has to be a limiting factor. That's what makes the holiday season so special for me. My childhood family gatherings consisted exclusively of aunts, uncles and cousins. It was a time for my brother and me to see our cousins who'd moved to California and another we'd not seen since a summer cookout at the lake. Holiday gatherings looked like a living, breathing family tree.

These days, though, my holiday gatherings are blended. As I look over the past few holiday seasons, I can point to several occasions in which good friends invited their very close friends to join them for the holidays. Many times, by the generosity of these good people, I've found my family on the receiving side of these invitations. These celebrations have joined those of my childhood in holiday memories I now hold dear. Not only have I been able to spend time with good friends, but I've had the privilege of making many new friends along the way.

Sociologists could probably attribute the shift to the growing transient nature of our society, as so many of us move around the country to follow our careers, but I'm not convinced. I'd rather believe that as we get older, we learn to assign the proper value to good friends.

Friends are special because we keep them by mutual commitment. Many times, the only link between the you and the person sitting across the Thanksgiving table is that you once lived in the same town together, or that they are the friend of a friend. But it isn't the link that matters – it's the connection. The holiday season is a time for us to open our homes, arms and hearts to those who make our life so rich and meaningful, and hey become family by dotted line.

As dear as I hold my childhood memories, these days I am thrilled to be able to reach out beyond the solid lines of my family tree and embrace those connected to me by the dotted lines of friendship. 'Tis the season to show love and appreciation -- don't miss the opportunity. ●

60 Grand Plan Awaits Parents

There is nothing in the world like being a parent. I've proudly said it for years.

The joy, the pain, the exhilaration, all wrapped up in an amazingly complex package beyond anything my heart ever dreamt. Until earlier this week, I unquestionably believed those emotions to be the exclusive territory of parents. But now I see hints of something else in the eyes of the people around me.

I was sharing stories with a friend whom I'd not seen in years. His own children grown, he shook my belief with his words.

"I guess that's why they call them 'grand' children," he said with a deep pride, like nothing I'd ever seen.

His grandchildren are the emotional center of his new world, and he was revealing a layer of emotion I'd never considered before that conversation. I can't personally speak to his experiences, but I do recognize the telltale ache in his voice when he talks about his grandchildren. His words are packaged in admiration and generously lavished with love. There is, when it comes to grandchildren, no rule of modesty — nor should there be. Grandparents have earned those rights.

My mother-in-law's bright blue eyes lit up whenever one of her grandchildren walked into her living room. It didn't matter how young or old they were — they were all unquestionably loved, and no visit by them could be long enough to satisfy her. From their side came the same strong emotions, revealing a secret bond held between two generations.

Time with my children seems to be slipping away too quickly. For years, I've carefully guarded my time with them, knowing each day I don't spend with them is one I won't get back. Each of those days is accompanied by a hollow ache in my heart. Being a parent is my calling in life, but after listening to my friend, I can take a breath and hope there someday might be another stage —equally unique and "grand" — out there on the horizon. ●

61 Hands Hold Meaning Beyond Obvious

Today I am counting days with a heavy heart.

Walking across a congested parking lot, holiday traffic swirling around us, my 10-year-old daughter instinctively reached up and took my hand. I closed my fingers protectively around her warm little hand, but my heart and mind were screaming out that these days are numbered.

She is quickly becoming a young woman, so I cherish those days she still reaches for me. Eventually, that instinct will conflict with her growing independence and there will come a day when she withdraws, stopped by a force neither of us can see and only one can feel. I know it's coming. I just hope I'm distracted enough not to recognize the moment, because I know how much it will hurt.

We are so eager to push our children into life — even bragging about how accelerated they are for their ages – only to one day find ourselves hoping to slow down the acceleration.

Holding hands with daughters is a treasured opportunity for fathers. Each parent has certain strengths and connections, and though my wife and I love our children equally, their first instinct is to go to mother. Me? Well, I'm a supporting cast member, relegated to running for bandages, wet paper towels, or ice cubes wrapped in a washcloth. I'd like to think I have the market cornered when they are scared but I've lived through enough midnight thunderstorms to know they're really just seeking the closest warm body.

But walking in a crowded department store or along a busy street — that's my domain. Holding hands starts out as protection for them from strangers, to prevent them getting lost or walking in front of moving traffic. These days, holding my daughter's hand in the parking lot is much more for my benefit than for hers. I dread the day her instincts fall to her independence and I no longer feel her hand slip up beneath mine as the traffic boils around us.

I want to think I'm prepared, but I know I'm not. It will be the closing of a major door in my role as a dad. Not that I won't be around for comfort and protection, but face it: Eventually, there will be an uninvited third party in the equation, separating my hand from hers. I look forward to a time when she and I can take a long walk together again, holding hands outside the influence of this pesky third party.

Only then, odds are, our roles will be reversed, and I'll be the one looking for comfort. ●

62 Holidays Mean Waisted Opportunities

The holidays are always a difficult for my waistline and me. Starting with Halloween -- okay, so my personal definition of the holidays might be a bit more encompassing than most -- I feel as if I'm on a two-month-long walk through a cornucopia of temptation. The food is just too good to resist.

This year has been more tempting than ever. After nearly a year on good terms with the scale in the corner of my bathroom, we are no longer speaking. Granted, I'm not being particularly mature about it, but sometimes we all need a time out.

After eating a piece of my son's birthday cake earlier this week, I was lamenting my current condition. My wife and kids realize that sometimes, telling little white lies can be an act of kindness. Love is a beautiful thing.

"Honey," my wife said, "you're being too hard on yourself. The holidays are to be enjoyed. You'll lose the weight quickly. You always do."

Our 15-year old son tossed a couple of cents' worth of compassion.

"Dad, you're not fat," he said. "Get over it."

Not to be outdone, our 10-year-old daughter joined in with her special blend of pity and in-your-face honesty.

"Dad," she said, her mouth full of cake. "If it bothers you

that much, just don't look down."

Ouch. Sometimes I'm not ready for her unique brand of stinging practicality. The next day, however, I began to appreciate her straightforwardness. I can learn from her.

But standing in the kitchen that particular night, I was not looking for honesty. I wanted comforting. I needed help dealing with the situation I'd put myself in by sampling from the delicious cornucopia all around me. What I needed to come to grips with was the present. You know, the one reflected by my former friend, the scale in the upstairs bathroom, earlier that day. And there is something incredibly humbling about giving up that extra notch on the belt. Forget symbolism – we're talking ego here.

Still stinging from my daughter's honesty, I'm coming to grips with my denial. There are times to let loose the reins, and good food and friends during the holidays are too important to let vanity get in the way. I have made the conscious decision not to let life slip away without my participation, one of the most fulfilling and far-reaching decisions in my life. The holidays are the crowning season for this philosophy.

But with respect to my health, I will continue to be careful and diligent for the sake of my family and me. There is nothing I hold more valuable than my time with them. As for my waistline, well, if I need to make a "January adjustment" to my belt, so be it. After all, if it bothers me that much I can heed my daughter's advice and just don't look down. ●

63 Child's Eyes Focus on Society's Inconsistency

Earlier this week, my 11-year-old challenged my personal values.

Sitting at a red light, she and I watched as a long white school bus crossed in front of us. Its back end, modified to transport tools and equipment, caught my daughter's attention.

"Who's on that bus?" she asked.

"Prisoners on work detail," I said.

"What do they do?"

"Clean up along the sides of the road and such."

"Why don't they just break through the windows and run away?"

"Because the guards would shoot them."

"But if they kill them, that's murder," she said with a frown.

My words seemed surreal as they came out of my mouth in the car that afternoon.

"Well, not really," I said, uncomfortable even as I spoke. "It's okay, according to the law."

"But isn't it against the law to murder someone?"

"Yes."

"Then why is it okay for them to shoot and kill someone?"

I felt as if I were standing on a sandbar, the waves of her words washing away my footing.

"You need to remember, some of the people in prison and jail committed some very bad crimes," I explained.

"But how does killing them make it better?" she protested. "By killing someone, aren't we making someone else angry, and then maybe they go out and kill someone? I mean, maybe if we'd quit killing people, other people might quit killing other people, too."

The sand between my toes continued to wash away as she continued to pepper me with questions.

"Why is it okay for some people to kill some people and not others?" she asked "Isn't murdering someone a sin?"

Her final wave crashed against me, and I was left with my two legs standing on opposite plots of moral ground.

She had landed a stinging blow to my core beliefs of right and wrong. How is it, she was asking me, that we can play by two sets of rules when it comes to a human life? I thought back to a time when I wrestled with the same question.

It was at the execution of a state prisoner. I stayed outside the protective walls of the facility, but a reporter from our newspaper was inside. A large crowd of people gathered around the prison entrance, some individuals holding candles or signs and some speaking into bullhorns. In the small sea of people, only their messages distinguished those who supported the death penalty from those who opposed it.

As temperatures dropped with the approach of midnight – the hour set for execution -- I found myself asking the very same questions my daughter was posing. It was that night, with the cold winds blowing around me, when I first questioned whether we as a society had the right to create a set of laws so dramatically inconsistent with the moral ground we claimed.

When word came that the prisoner was dead, the crowd dispersed. Media vans closed up, protesters folded their signs under their arms and bullhorn debates ended. My daughter's words touched on an intensely personal conflict I have battled for years, my first doubts about legislating life and death emerging as I stood in the cold beside the white walls of a state prison. I guess I just needed an 11-year-old to remind me I have yet to honestly settle the question myself. ●

64 Friendship in a Flattening World

"I remember as a kid when a neighbor would move away and it would be like they'd fallen off the face of the earth," my friend said, speaking to me through a cell phone. "They could've just moved across town or across state, but you never saw or heard from them again."

He is talking about how flat the world has become.

In Thomas Friedman's book, *The World Is Flat: A Brief History of the Twenty-first Century*, he lays out a compelling case for the way technology is radically changing the landscape of global business and communication. With the advent of e-commerce, racing through fiber-optic cables buried beneath the ocean floors, our world is changing in dimensions we could never envision only a decade ago. The world, according to Friedman's theory, is becoming a place where communication is oblivious to national borders or distances.

As I listened to my friend reminiscing about the very different world we grew up in, I recognized Friedman's theory beginning to bear fruit in my own friends and children.

Recently our family was in the middle of a long-distance move, experiencing all the mixed emotions inherent in the process. Leaving behind good friends is never easy. Most of us go through life meeting thousands of people, but regarding very few our friends. Despite our best intentions, we find distance and time difficult hurdles to consistently overcome. Life gets busy. A new home brings new acquaintances and experiences. The equation changes on both sides.

But there is a new world of friendship buoyed by technology. No longer does moving across town mean losing contact with people who mean so much to you. And I only need to look to my children to better understand this trend.

I remember being my daughter's age and having a neighbor move out of state. We all knew what to expect. He might as well have been moving to China. Not only did we lack access to easy communication tools, but our social skills lagged behind those of children today. The only flattening tools we could use were a postage stamp or long-distance telephone call, and those cost money.

Today I watch as my children accept and use this new flattening world not only to keep in touch, but also to extend their already wide range of friendships. With low-cost and easy-to-access tools such as e-mail and instant messenger applications, I see them amass large networks of friends, regardless of zip code or time zone. It is not uncommon for me to look over my children's shoulders and see them speaking with friends nearly a thousand miles away, the same as if they lived around the corner.

The world, as Friedman points out, is indeed flattening. We are entering a world in which moving down the block — or to China — will no longer be a barrier to keeping friendships alive. ●

65 Lapel Pin Speaks Volumes

My friend's small, nondescript lapel pin speaks volumes. "Attitude," it silently shouts, "is everything."

The two of us were sitting across from each other in a community meeting the first time his pin, the size of a dime, captured my imagination. I've always respected the philosophy that a positive attitude's ability can move mountains, and I found it refreshing that he openly promoted his personal attitude with everyone he met. For him, success is not an accident but a result of how we address the world around us every day. He greets everyone warmly, like a long-time friend and he welcomes each opportunity to make a difference for the good. In every disappointment, he looks for a lesson to take away and use productively in the future.

My friend, retired from a local school system, remains a great teacher.

Throughout my life I've met literally of individuals from countless backgrounds and professions. My contact with some can be measured in minutes, and some I get to know well. But the one thing I always look for beneath the professional exteriors is their true heartbeats — their attitudes.

The other day, my 15-year-old son and I were discussing this very subject.

"Be careful of people who are quick to find the negative in everything," I said.

He is mature and able to make good decisions on his own,

but this is a lesson I believe can never be shared too often.

"At the end of the day, those whose first instinct is to complain or find fault will be left holding a big bag of complaints," I told him. "But it's an illusion. There's nothing there. In the meantime, those who are working hard will have already made a difference and moved on."

Later that week, coincidentally, I found myself testifying to a coworker about why I share my friend's lapel-pin philosophy.

"When I was growing up, only a few miles from Arrowhead Stadium in Kansas City, no one could strike fear in the heart of a Chiefs' fan like John Elway of the Denver Broncos," I said. "If left with less than two minutes on the clock, he repeatedly would march his team down the field and snatch the game away from us. He did it more times than I can even remember. You know why? Not because he was the greatest quarterback of all time, but because when he had the ball and the game on the line he fully expected to score and win the game. And because he believed, his teammates believed. He had the skills, but more importantly, he believed he and his team would score. And that attitude made all the difference in the world to his teammates."

So as I continue to find myself learning from others, I can't help but think about how much my friend — a retired teacher of students — and a Hall of Fame quarterback share in common. For both men, their secret to success in life can be summed up in a simple phrase modestly displayed on a lapel pin.●

66 Good China is Best When Used

The best advice sometimes arrives from the most unexpected places.

"So," said the elderly woman. "Just who are saving your good china for – his next wife?"

Inside a beautiful old jewelry store, speaking with an equally beautiful 90-year-old woman, my wife and I found our lives changed forever by a random conversation.

The woman's comment – the wisdom hidden inside her statement - deeply resonate within my wife and me many years later. Life, she was telling us, is to be enjoyed, not wrapped in tissue and hidden away in a cardboard box, waiting for the perfect time to arrive. The conversation began with our china and how often we use it. Somewhat sheepishly, my wife admitted she'd kept it protected and stored away since our wedding. Children, moving – all our excuses seemed reasonable until they came under the scrutiny of this 90-year-old woman.

Years have passed, and still my wife and I continue to incorporate her philosophy into our daily life. Things, we now know, are just things. You can touch them. You can break them. You can replace them. Opportunity, on the other hand, is intangible. We cannot touch it, replace it and safely store it away in a box to use later. Practicing this philosophy requires always being on the lookout for the chance to live the moment.

A couple of weeks ago, daffodils began to break through the ground in our front yard. Walking outside to collect the morning newspaper, I paused to notice how the yellow flowers dramatically brightened up an otherwise colorless yard. With the late winter breeze sweeping around me, I reached down and picked one, then carried it into our house.

There was a time when I'd have hesitated to pick the first and only sign of spring, but I now understand our "china" cannot be fully enjoyed when it is wrapped and stored away in the attic. You see, by capturing spring and placing the flower in a small vase in our kitchen, I was practicing the philosophy of living my life in the now.

Life requires a great deal of planning and self-restraint, yes, but we can all learn from 90 years of experience. The woman in the jewelry store had lost her husband long ago, yet lovingly spoke of him as if he were still just around the corner, repairing a pocket watch for a regular customer. She'd learned long ago life is not an infinite run. Plans can and should be made, but not if living in the future costs us the experiences of the now. For the now, her words taught us, is where life is lived. It is where joy lifts us up, where pain stings us, where our memories are etched permanently inside our hearts.

Where is your "china?" Find it. Use it. Don't put your heart on hold. Life is to be lived and enjoyed. Someday does not come with a lifetime of memories unless you allow yourself to learn from 90 years of experience. ●

67 Immigration Issue Touches Core Values

At 21, my mother sold everything she owned to finance a one-way ticket across the Atlantic Ocean in pursuit of the American Dream.

As a child during the second world war, my mother's dream was to raise her own children in America, away from a politically unstable and war-torn Europe. She shared stories across the breakfast table with my younger brother and me, the memories and emotions of her childhood painfully close to the surface even though decades and 3,000 miles separated her from her native Scotland by that time.

For immigrants, an American Dream is as unique as their individual fingerprints. My mother's story, which is not unlike millions of others, gives me pause when I am trying to better understand the immigration issues we face in the United States today. I view myself, along with the family my wife and I have created, fulfillment of my mother's dream. Who am I, then, to turn away those seeking their own version of that dream?

Current estimates show more than 11 million illegal aliens residing in the United States. That equals the entire metropolitan areas of Atlanta, Phoenix and St. Louis combined. Think about that for a moment. That's how big a problem our nation is attempting to wrap its arms around right now.

I can't help but remember the small United States flag presented to my mother on the day she earned her American citizenship. To become a naturalized citizen, she was required first to apply for citizenship, then to pass a battery of tests to demonstrate she knew our country's history and had at least a basic understanding of how our government operates. My mother's citizenship required a promise of commitment and contribution to society, and she cherished that flag as though it were a priceless family jewel.

So while I can appreciate the strong desire to come to America, I'm torn over illegal immigration, knowing the commitment so many have made – and still make – to legally immigrate to this country. I want to find a way to welcome all, but I can't fully support those who blatantly ignore the laws others so carefully follow to gain entry to America. What troubles me is, regardless of my respect for any immigrant who significantly contributes to society, I cannot welcome the presence of at least 11 million immigrants without ignoring the laws we, as citizens, are expected to uphold.

America. Its prosperity, generosity and compassion is a testament to God's grace here on earth. It is no wonder that so many people wish to walk though its doors in pursuit of their version of the American Dream. It is these very values we as a nation need to apply to resolve the large-looming issue of immigration. The United States always will be in debt to immigrants, to their great courage and contributions. What we must now do now is use the best characteristics of our America – the ones that continues to draw immigrants to her – and figure out a way to welcome the new without disrespecting those who've legally come before them. ●

68 Snow Angels Trump Currency

One gift my daughter continues to remind me of is that life — if we give it the chance — is a heck of a lot of fun.

While I was away for a couple of days, winter arrived early back home. My daughter told me I'd missed the first snow of the season, then paused and got down to business.

"So, how much if I shovel the driveway?" she asked.

With my 10-year-old, everything is negotiable. Not that she's really all that concerned with the outcome, but she certainly enjoys the give-and-take of the game.

"How about $5?" I said.

"How about $20?" she countered.

"How about $4?" I said, steering away from her higher price.

"OK, I'll do it for $10," she said, assuming the close, then quickly changed the conversation.

Somewhere beyond her age, we seem to get caught up in the serious pursuits of life. Not that isn't necessary, but every now and then it's nice to be reminded we shouldn't ignore the roads less traveled in front of us each day.

On the telephone the next night, I asked my wife if our daughter did a good job shoveling the driveway.

"Well, that's an interesting story," she said. "There seems to be one long stripe down the right side of the driveway and a several snow angels. Also, it looks like she's been throwing snowballs at her brother's window."

I couldn't hide my smile, knowing how much this girl just loves life. I realize I've unintentionally hardened through time and experience. Responsibility insists upon it after all. But occasionally, as children seem to see with little difficulty, life presents an opportunity for us to explore. And as an adult I value these lessons I can learn from my children.

In the big picture of things, is it really a big deal that my daughter never finished shoveling the driveway? Honestly, no. How much of a challenge can two inches of snow on a gently inclining driveway present for a 5,000-pound, all-wheel-drive SUV? And how can I be upset that my daughter has the unique gift of being able to see the snow angels' secret hiding place beneath a white blanket of snow? We adults may believe we have all the answers, but we need to realize sometimes we just don't have our children's vision or their ability to see beyond the obvious.

Snow eventually melts and dollars are spent on items soon discarded or forgotten. Memories, on the other hand, are the currency of life. Spend wisely. ●

69 Ornaments Display Memories

"Please don't eat me."

This little request, written on the reverse side of a brown Styrofoam gingerbread man ornament, reminds my wife and me of a particular year we could not keep our newly mobile baby daughter from putting him in her mouth every time we turned away from the Christmas tree.

I'm sure we're like a lot of people, each year selecting an ornament for our tree to mark the time. To be honest, though, I needed to be coaxed into this particular tradition 23 years ago when my wife and I first met.

"How about this one?" she said, holding up a red glass ornament during a July sidewalk sale.

"What for?" I asked, not sure why she would want to purchase a Christmas ornament in the middle of summer.

"Each year you pick a new one to hang on the tree and after a while you've a tree full of memories," she explained.

I'll admit, I probably bought it more for its clearance-table price than for her sentimental plan at the time. But now, that ornament is yet another reminder of why I needed this woman in my life.

Even though nearly two dozen years' worth of memories dangle from our tree each Christmas, our entire family still eagerly anticipates the ceremonial placing of ornaments on limbs. Carefully unpacking them and hanging them in chronological order, we tell stories of the years they represent, the kids sometimes adding details we've forgotten from the previous year's telling. With the stories come a rush of memories hidden below the rush of our everyday lives.

My wife will say, "1994," holding up an ornament, as the kids race each other for a chance to hang that one from an available branch. And with each we informally pass along another part of our family history.

Apologies to our good friends at Hallmark, but a majority of these ornaments are of a much more personal nature. Some are paper cutouts and almost all have the date hand-written on them, as opposed to the mass-produced variety of dated models.

"Remember this one?" my wife asked the other morning, touching a small plastic piece with a tiny cottage painted on it. "I bought this one from a man selling ornaments for the blind in a parking lot in Pittsburgh."

Looking at our tree, I can see an expectant mother figure from the year our son was born, along with a wooden cutout of a couple holding hands. The year 1985 is marked on the back in gold glitter pen.

Over the years, standard-issue ornaments — fabric-covered baubles in red, green and gold — have found it more difficult to make it out of their boxes as they are displaced by our memories. Reflecting our Christmas tradition, our kids began selecting an ornament for themselves in each of the past several years, further making limb space a premium. More stories to remember, more stories to tell.

So should you one day catch sight of our Christmas tree and notice the absence of more traditional decorations, remember this: To us, there is much more to the tree than any naked eye could ever hope to see. ●

70 Permit Opens a New Door for Parents

Very few rites of passage loom larger than the driver's permit bestowed on my 15-year-old son by the state earlier this week.

"Wow," I said to my wife. "This feels really weird."

Looking down at the card, seeing his name printed beside his photo, I suddenly felt as if my little boy was gone forever. Proudly secured atop his money clip, that driver's permit is the first official recognition of his accelerating maturity from the world outside his family.

Holding the small card in my fingers, I couldn't help but think of when I first met him on a cold, snowy winter morning. His eyes, eagerly searching the world around him, made contact with mine for the very first time. At that moment, my world stopped as the child that occupied my body voluntarily exited, the adult in charge without a fight. Never had I seen the future more clearly than I did when I first introduced myself to my son.

I returned the permit to my son, and, his face proud, he placed it into his pocket and left me alone in the room with my thoughts. Sure, I knew this day would arrive, but surely it would be further down the line. Parents with teenagers who drive are much older. How could this be?

My son is oblivious to the fact that this is a brand new world for me, one filled with a brand-new set of fears. Until now, he's spent the majority of his life within arm's length of me.

Now, on the cusp of the new freedom the state is extending to him, he will be free to travel far beyond the reach of my protective cocoon. Until now, his travel experience was dependent on my driving him. With his newfound freedom, he'll literally be the one with his hands on the steering wheel.

Furthermore I have a suddenly powerful appreciation for the concerns countless parents face at this threshold. In the hundreds of thousands of miles I've driven over the years, I've come to accept the fact that my safety is not necessarily in my hands. That lesson came home to me one recent morning when an SUV lost control and crossed into my lane. With my dad's words of caution -- "Always drive defensively, son. You never know what the other guy is going to do." – echoing in my head, I braced myself for the impact of metal on metal. By the grace of God, the other vehicle regained control just before our vehicles would've met.

I was a teenager full of testosterone with a tank full of high-octane gasoline a V-8 engine, I thought that would be enough to help me avoid any possible danger my dad could warn me about. Boy, how my perspective has changed, now that I have a few years and a handful of grey hair to look back over. I guess I'm just at the point in life all parents eventually find themselves, realizing their children are, well, no longer children. ●

71 Technology Facilitates Time Travel

Through the magic of technology I've been going back in time.

Recently my dad began scanning and cataloging old family photos in his home computer. Armed with a simple desktop scanner and an oversize monitor, he's now sending out daily e-mails to my younger brother and me. He labels them with cryptic subject lines designed to pique our interest.

This week, he unearthed an old box of my late mother's family photos, and with it came a peek into a world I've never experienced before. "Four Princesses" opened up to a black-and-white photo of my mother and her three older sisters standing in front of the cottage where they lived before the second world war broke out in Europe. Another arrived today with a photo of a grandfather I never met sitting at a small table in what appears to be an old pub. His preoccupied glance - he is looking away from the camera - leaves me aching to ask him what he's thinking about.

But the one I can't get of my mind isn't a photo at all. Earlier this week, "A Lifetime of Addresses" arrived in my inbox, and with it, a flood of emotions I never expected to feel. I read a hand-written listing of all the places my mother called home in her relatively short lifetime. Looking closer at the image of a browning sheet of paper emanating from my computer screen, I recognized her penmanship, something I'd never thought of as distinctive when I was a child. There are 26 letters in the alphabet but the unique formation of her "G" betrayed her European schooling.

Each listing began with the number of years, her complete name, the address, city / town, and county. One address, listed only as "Bridge Cottage, Furnace, Argyll, Scotland" is detailed with the number 8, indicating how long she lived there. Remarkably, she continued her list by cataloging the hopscotch of addresses where she lived during the war years, a time at which she and her sisters were separated during efforts to keep entire families from being wiped out in German bombing raids.

Each listing brings another flood of memories, and I can almost hear her voice telling me the stories of her life. The voice I hear today is real, only it speaks from my heart. With this innocent little project of my father's, I'm going back to a time I thought I'd comfortably filed away under "memories for another day." With each arrival a box of dormant memories reopens and I'm awash in warm and powerful emotions as I travel back in time.

I'm learning is time travel is as easy as my reflections on what I already know in my heart. That and a little help from technology remind me what is hidden away in my box of memories. ●

72 Bypassing Bypass Revealing

Sometimes getting lost is just what we need.

While driving through a nearby state last week, I decided my printed directions were no longer doing anything but confusing me. Frustrated, I chucked them onto the back seat and vowed to find my own way using only my instincts and state-issued road signs.

As most of us know from experience, this was not a foolproof plan. Within minutes I was pulling off the interstate and onto a two-lane state road winding through towering pine trees. A green sign with white lettering directed me away from the comfort of the high-speed interstate and invited me to travel its quiet roads at a greatly reduced pace.

Slowing down as I entered a small town, I spotted a sign advertising gasoline for $1.42 per gallon – and the tall weeds which had long ago taken ownership of the property. A weathered sign with a single phone number hung from the door. The sorry state of that business was a testament to the magnetic draw of the interstate for its travelers. Here, a half-dozen miles away may as well be thousand.

Further down the road, I saw a sprawling factory with only a smattering of cars parked in its oversized lot. Located on the main road leading into town, the factory reminded me of a time when industry was a community's centerpiece, proudly displayed for all to see.

Another state sign pointed me to the left as I approached a stoplight. Across the intersection, a dozen or so people milled around in front of a vegetable stand offering "Sweet Potatoes/Too for a $." The light changed. I waited, and no one honked.

Becoming more familiar with my surroundings, I realized the town was void of even the most common chain restaurants. A sign invited me to try a barbecue sandwich. The time is always right for good barbecue, so I pulled in. An employee approached the counter as I entered the door.

"Hello," she said. "You ever eaten here before – 'cause there are no refunds."

That took me aback.

She handed me a small paper cup, a fork and a mustard-colored sample, then crossed her arms across her chest.

"Interesting," I said after sampling. "Sign me up."

Silently she turned, deftly wrapping a sandwich in silver foil and plopping it on an orange tray.

"Five-dollars, thirty-nine cents," she announced.

I traded my money for the tray and took a seat near the door. The Sons of the Confederate Soldiers invited me to join their organization, according to a pamphlet on my table and each of the other half-dozen tables in that fine establishment. The pamphlets were competing with a faded photocopy of the Constitution of the United States for my attention.

For the next 15 minutes, I was observing a world where the counter help calls everyone by name as they walk in the door. I finished my sandwich, which was really pretty good, returned my tray to the counter and walked back to my car. A half-hour later I rediscovered the interstate and put my bypass into the past -- behind me, but not forgotten. ●

73 Children Silently Shed Childhood

"So, do you have kids?"

With our son on the cusp of 16 and our daughter racing toward 12, my wife and I are finding the term "kids" increasingly inadequate. The age of innocence quickly is fading into the background and maturity silently but insistently is nudging in, and we're not exactly sure where the line between the two stops.

This is an extremely unnerving but well-traveled crossroads for parents. Only now, my wife and I are the ones watching another stage of life unfolding before us.

For years our standard answer to such an innocuous question could be, "Yes, a son, 9, and a daughter, 5." Simple question, just insert current ages. This worked faithfully for years as a great conversation starter with other parents. That is, until recently. The day you recognize your children as young adults you begin to visualize an invisible - yet curiously tangible - threshold between childhood and teenage years.

I'm happy they are growing up, really. What I'm wrestling with is the increasing speed at which they seem to be doing it.

"You know you're growing up pretty fast now," I said to my daughter the other day as we drove to school.

Looking up from her backpack, she flashed me a brilliant smile, one of satisfaction. She knows she is on her way and there is nothing I can do stop it. Just a couple of years ago, I remember sharing dinner with a couple we were just getting to know when the subject of children floated across the table. As usual my wife grabbed it, inserted the current ages, and returned the question.

"Well," he said, almost apologetically. "We have a pair of teenagers."

I remember wondering why they made they made the distinction. After all, we're only talking about a couple years, right?

Today I understand what he meant. Granted, your offspring will always be your children, but at some point "children" seems an inaccurate way to describe them. While "child" generally is considered a small, dependent stage, "teenager" carries an entirely different set of expectations. As a parent, you find yourself increasingly letting out additional lengths of ropes of responsibility. Trust becomes a bit more than hoping they don't spill a drink in the living room.

A couple of months ago I spoke again with the friend who first made that crucial distinction between "child" and "teenager."

"Funny thing happened when we got home that year," he said. "We discovered there'd been a party at our home that weekend. Kind of a Beanstock-type event (his last name is Bean). Nothing broken, but a party all the same."

As he laughed across the phone line, the event well behind him and his kids now college graduates, I couldn't help but feel anxiety over the unknown growing in me.

"Just you wait," he said. "You just raise them the best you can and hope they'll remember your guidance when you're not around."

So today, with our children's childhood fading into the past, I'm discovering there is more to maturity than the number of candles on the birthday cake. Something, I believe, I'm on the very front edge of learning. Wish me luck. ●

74　How Thirsty Are You?

I recently asked a coworker if she'd prefer Coke or Pepsi — and it had nothing to do with a drink.

Years ago, someone told me a great way to get down to the wick of someone's personality is to pose the following question: "If you were applying for a sales representative job in a town where Coke owned a 95 percent market share and Pepsi held only 5 percent, which would you like to work for?"

I remember thinking, "What's the big deal about this? Easy choice for most people…"

"Here's how it works," he said. "The key is in the answer."

I was pretty young at the time, only a few years out of college, but I knew enough to wait to hear his logic on the subject.

"There is no right or wrong answer, but it tells you volumes about someone's attitudes."

He paused and let me think a bit more about the question.

"Well, what do you think?" he said.

Showing great mentoring skills, he stepped into answer precisely between the moment I'd made my choice and actually said it aloud.

"Like I said, for the person answering there is not a right

or wrong answer to the question, but the answer gives you a hint of what is inside," he said.

I was confused.

"If you answered 'Coke' it tells me you just might be someone not particularly comfortable with intense competition and might be more comfortable in a predictable, stable environment," he explained. "On the other hand, answering 'Pepsi' might lead me to believe you're more of a risk taker, someone who sees the opportunity to challenge a competitor and find out what you're really made of."

I thought about my answer — and then his reasoning.

"Think about it," he continued. "How much opportunity is there for the guy selling Coke to increase his market share? How reasonable is it to expect Coke to grab a 100 percent market share? Heck, you're setting yourself up for maintenance at best. The other guy, Pepsi, well there's the opportunity. If he takes the Pepsi market share from 5 to 10 percent he'd doubled his sales and market penetration, and against a Goliath of a competitor. He's a hero. Imagine how his resume and reputation is going to look after a while?"

Years later, long after he coached me up and out of his organization, I still find myself drawing on his advice. As opportunities presented themselves in the following years I found myself looking back to his simple analogy and asking myself what I want my career to reflect years down the line.

So, who are you? Coke or Pepsi? ●

75 Parents Teach Ropes in Life

A few pages into a new book I'd begun reading, I came to an abrupt halt.

"Integrity," read the sentence that stopped me cold, "is doing the right thing when no one is looking."

The words, so succinct and without pretense, froze me in my tracks.

As parents, we all focus on teaching our children the ropes in life: honesty, hard work, respect for others and how to truly love someone with all your heart. We hope by sharing these tools with them they will one day find happiness and success in life.

The next day, still excited about the amazingly clear passage I'd read the night before, I shared it with a friend.

As I repeated the phrase I could see a smile cross his face.

"You know," he said, "my dad used to repeatedly say the very same thing to me growing up."

He warmly recalled those talks with his father.

"What surprises me," he continued, "is that not everyone teaches his or her children that very same principle."

I thought about it for a moment, how fortunate he was for his father to drill such a lesson into him – a lesson that helped create the successful adult his son has become.

The lessons of our childhood, I believe, are the driving

force of making us who and what we are as adults. Although the role of disciplinarian can be difficult at times for parents and children, I now recognize how these incidents in my childhood continue to pay dividends now that I'm an adult.

Reading the passage it helped resurrect a memory of when my mother, a switch, and a small piece of candy taught me a very valuable lesson about honesty.

"Where did you get that piece of candy?" she asked me one day when I was not yet old enough to start kindergarten. My lessons were still being taught exclusively at home back then, and mostly by my mother.

"In the bin at the grocery store, " I answered.

"Did you pay for it?" she asked, knowing I barely understood the concept of money.

"No," I said.

The next short while is a blur – probably for obvious reasons – but I do remember her dragging me up to the corner grocer, making me hand over the candy and apologizing to the man who owned the store. To this day, I remember how badly I felt about what I'd done, innocently or not. Did the piece of penny candy threaten his store's profitability? Could my mother have easily paid him for it? Probably. But that day I learned there are certain lines in life we are never to cross. And in the home where I grew up, honesty was non-negotiable.

Much like my friend's dad taught integrity, my wife and I are teaching the lessons of our youth. In particular, we've always told our children that telling the truth and paying for your actions are two different things.

I guess what I learned from the book and from my friend is that even though some parents may use a different script, they're teaching from the heart and doing the very best they can. Even when they know no one is looking. ●

76 Playing Back Nine is Emotional

Recently I've been waking up every morning feeling as if I'm walking the back nine of life with our two children with only a couple of holes remaining to play.

Our son, now 15, and daughter, 11, always seemed as if they were "children," but now that they are headed toward young adulthood, I can almost see the final holes up ahead. And that scares the daylights out of me.

Saturday mornings generally are laid back in our home. The kids tend to sleep late after watching movies the night before and my wife and I share coffee over morning newspapers. Eventually I'll slide out and work around the yard for a bit, or maybe run a few errands before the kids get going for the day. More frequently now, my first thoughts on Saturday are reminders that in a few short years, the house will be much quieter.

Don't get me wrong. I'm excited for them, as this is the natural progression of maturity. Preparing them to leave is all about making sure they have the tools and knowledge to successfully navigate life on their own. What's missing is my emotional preparation for overseeing an empty nest.

"Enjoy them while you can," said a friend recently. "They grow up so fast you won't believe it."

I found a certain irony in his words, as he'd just inquired about the ages of my children and I know his are now college graduates, married and living away from his home. There is still time for me, from his perspective.

But time, it turns out, is not all I need. I need an "in" into their lives. With each developing interest outside my world, I find it increasingly more difficult to find a way into their worlds. More and more as I walk past their rooms, I find them immersed in a universe of computers, cell phones and games. No longer are they dependent on me to find something to do. Rather, their growing independence actually forces my intrusions to be more calculated, attractive. Accompanying me on a grocery store run is losing its allure.

Time marches on, and so do they. While they race ahead, I'm slow-walking, learning to take in the scenery around me. After walking with them hand-in-hand for years, I can feel an internal time clock ticking away as they excitedly pull away whenever a new mile marker appears ahead.

The average child lives at home until around 18, same as the number of holes on a golf course. Using that analogy I'm deep into the back nine with my son. The trick is to be sure I make the most of every moment during the final few holes. ●

77 Religion Policy Dangerous

Nothing seems more threatening than being alone in the dark, surrounded by noises you can't recognize.

So, I find myself asking more often, why don't we teach religion in public schools?

While driving the other day, a friend I began to talk about religion and the role it now plays in our everyday life.

"I mean," I protested, "growing up, I don't think ever knew what religion my neighbors were. They were just our neighbors. It's not that we didn't talk about it, it just wasn't a big deal."

The world of today is much different. Today I find myself regularly talking with my children about the different beliefs and values of religions not only around the corner, but also halfway across the globe.

Not that it is a "big deal" even now, just that it now plays a more integral role in the events surrounding us each day.

If we say we are sending our children to school for an education designed to prepare them for entering the global work-place, then why not actively teach them about the religions on the world? With each leap in technology, the world is getting smaller

-- and we had better figure out how to get along.

For the most part, the great religions of the world practice many of the same principles: respect, honor, honesty, helping others. So why do we insist on creating a shroud of mystery by refusing to allow our children to obtain a better understanding the world around them? After all, human nature is to fear what it fails to understand. Could it be said we are potentially creating a climate of intolerance through ignorance?

While I understand the historical position for the separation church and state in the United States, I'm not so sure the intent was to never mention God inside the four walls of a schoolhouse. On the contrary, I believe our nation should be a place where the free exchange of ideas is a well-respected practice, a place where God and religion also sit at our tables.

Today's headlines are full of events stained with the blood of religious intolerance. And intolerance is bred, in many cases, through ignorance. Man is a spiritual being, and to suppress this instinct is akin to taking a fish out of water. Without it we find ourselves struggling and gasping for something we know we need but can't find.

A few years ago I had the opportunity to listen to the great author Elie Wiesel speak to a community. Wiesel personally experienced one of man's worst horrors – the Holocaust – and his book "Night" is a terrifying journey for its readers.

"We should not be tolerant, as tolerance is to put up with," he said. "We should, rather, seek to understand."

Wiesel is a thin, frail man, but his words towered over the room. I've never been the same since hearing them.

Understanding comes from first being exposed to different points of view and beliefs, then examining that exposure with critical – yet meaningful – discussion. Let's bring religion back into the classroom and prepare our children for the real world. ●

78 Soundtrack of War Never Changes

War is hell, especially for children.

My wife's friend is working with Lebanese evacuees at the local airport.

"They were there at 3 a.m. to receive families and help watch over the children," my wife said, describing her friend's task. "She said they were there to help corral the children as the parents filled out paperwork."

Standing in our kitchen, I remembered the small faces I had seen on the television the night before, as rockets crisscross the border between southern Lebanon and northern Israel. As I listened to my wife, I pictured the families landing in the United States, most with only the clothes on their back to their name.

"They'd take photographs of the children with their parents so they'd be able to match them up afterwards," my wife added.

Apparently her friend's group set up an area to keep the kids occupied while the parents signed documents with officials. I knew they'd do their best to make the children feel comfortable, but not even thousands of miles could put their memories of war behind them.

"There was a man making balloon animals," my wife said. "But every once in awhile, one would pop and some of the smaller children would start to cry."

I couldn't help but think how unsettling is must be for all those young children. Granted, they are fortunate to now be in a safe haven, but I bet if you asked them, they'd say they would much rather be at home. The home of two months ago, that is. War is as ugly as man gets. We might be blessed with compassion and empathy for our fellow man, but history proves how quickly we can put out efforts into destruction instead. No doubt about it, man is good at making war.

It pains me to think of these small children entering airports across our nation as refugees instead of immigrants. I think of the conditions they've left behind, the rumble of jets flying over at night, the tremors of explosions in the distance. The soundtrack, for children, never changes over time. Innocent of ideology, they are left to try and make sense of a world literally turned upside down.

I wonder. Will these children ever hear a balloon pop and not instinctively jump? I remember how the Fourth of July always put my mother on edge. Because she grew up in Europe during World War II, fireworks affected her in a way my younger brother and I could not appreciate. Firecrackers, in particular, were too close to her memories and she'd always quietly slip inside the house until my brother and I finished our auditory celebration.

As our nation receives the neatly termed "collateral damage" of this war, I can't get my mother's face out of my mind. War may change location, but for the children of war everywhere, the soundtrack remains the same. ●

79 Gas Tank Filled With Memories

Driving along a winding back road earlier this week, I found myself approaching a small town. The only notice I'd given it in past drives was to take note of how many more miles I had to drive to get home from there.

As I passed beneath the single blinking yellow light in the center of town, my gas gauge recommended I find a place to re-fill. I noticed a small, well-worn gas station just down the road on the left, so I pulled into its driveway and stopped in front of the pump. I was just getting out of the car when a man walked out towards me. I was the only car at the station, so I thought maybe there was a problem with the pump.

"Good morning," I said. "Something wrong?"

Wearing a blue jumpsuit and moving with purpose, the man reached over, dislodged the nozzle and positioned it in my tank.

"No sir," he replied. "Just here to pump your gas. How much would you like?"

I came of age long after full-service filling stations disappeared, so I wasn't quite sure what I should do. I fumbled for an answer to his simple question. Suddenly, the days of sitting in the back seat of my dad's Oldsmobile sedan came back to me and I found the right words.

"Fill 'er up, please."

As the old stainless steel pump rhythmically worked, I realized I was lost again. No place to slide my credit card, no signs inviting me in for an ice-cold 64-once drink.

"Well," I said awkwardly, "I think I'll just step inside if that's okay with you."

I checked out the plate-glass window on the left and the small service bay on the right, a classic design built by the tens of thousands in decades past. These days, they've been replaced by modern one-stop convenience stores that also happen to offer gasoline. Opening the aluminum-framed door, I saw an old desk to my left and a small, refrigerated drink unit against the back wall. The station's modest original design had no room for long rows of fountain drinks and cappuccino machines.

Looking back outside at the man pumping my gas in the midday heat, I let a flow of old memories work their way back. Suddenly, I was looking out from the back seat of my dad's car at the dishes stations once gave away with a fill-up, and my mom making sure we completed our set. White cups with red stripes. And that time on vacation when the attendant handed my brother and me kites with the logo of his station on them. Phillips 66.

Lost in the past in a small room where the air moved with the help of a single metal fan, I returned from my daydream when the attendant completed his task and walked back in out of the heat. I paid for my gas and a bottle of cold water but considered it a bargain. For the price of a tank of gasoline, I had revisited a time when a service station provided just that – service. ●

80 Newlyweds Redefine Term

"Guess how old I am."

The neatly dressed older man, his wife standing beside him, is serious as he makes his request of me. I was visiting my aunt in her retirement home and had joined her and some friends for a pancake breakfast.

The man adjusts his posture, standing perfectly upright. His clothes are clean and classic. His bright eyes reflect an energetic and youthful spirit, making my challenge all the more difficult.

"Seventy?" I guess.

His face beams, and his wife smiles along with him.

"Nope," he says triumphantly. "Try 87."

As polite as my guess might have been, I'm honestly surprised at the age his driver's license confirms. In appearance, he easily is a decade younger. Gesturing at his wife, the man continues.

"How about her?"

This is not good. Regardless of the game we've been playing, I know better. It is obvious how much she cares for her husband, but equally obvious that she didn't expect this subject to come up over a pancakes and bacon.

"Really," he insists. "Guess."

I opt to give both his wife and me a comfortable out, I offer the number my mother always suggested: 29. She smiles, understanding my answer.

"Nope," he said. "Would you believe she's older than me?"

She playfully tugs at his arm as he shoots a sly look at her, encouraging her to come clean.

"A lady never tells," she says, politely – yet firmly – ending his game.

For the next few minutes we get the opportunity to know each other better, as they share stories of their lives, their children and the spouses they've buried. They each deeply love those they've lost. These two are, however, newlyweds.

"Got married last March," he says. "Pretty much had to talk her into marrying me."

It is just at moments like this I am reminded how full life can be for anyone who chooses to embrace the opportunities around them. Here is a couple, each widowed, who only recently came to know each other, only to find themselves in love in their later years. They are living a new chapter of life they couldn't have envisioned 25 years earlier.

The man pushes himself up from the table, balancing on two new hips. His wife, wearing an elegant fur vest trimmed in glittering stones, joins him. She is his princess, he her prince.

"Well, we should be going," he says.

I rise, shaking hands with each, and they turn towards the door. His right arm instinctively opens and her left arm gently slides through.

They are young, younger than most. Youth, I'm learning, is not measured by a birth certificate but by a combination of heart and mind. Together, these two are as young as any newlywed couple you'd ever meet. What they've found is that outliving a spouse doesn't necessarily mean outliving love. Somehow, some way, their paths crossed for a reason. They respect and understand their places in life, and what they're not ready to do is quit living when love knocks at the door. ●

81 Painful Decision Based on Love

"At some point, families need to decide if they are keeping the person alive for themselves or the family member," the caller quietly said.

I had been sitting on my living room sofa, praying for guidance in dealing with the steadily deteriorating condition of my aunt, when the phone rang. A minister from Arizona, someone I'd met only once, had called to see how I was coping with my aunt's medical power of attorney. The call reminded me how the hand of God is always with us, whether we recognize it or not.

Her voice was a buoy in a sea of medical opinions. For weeks I'd attempted to balance my lack of experience with serious medical conditions and life-altering decisions for my aunt. Regardless of the answers to my questions, I researched terms and quietly cornered nurses to better understand what the doctor's calculated statements really meant.

"This isn't an easy situation for anyone," the minister said. "But you've just got to do what you believe in your heart your aunt would want you to do." Her voice was strong, yet compassionate.

She'd undoubtedly faced this situation countless times, but she had called not to direct me, only to help me find my own way through. And my situation wasn't an unusual one. Every day, families find themselves making medical decisions neither they nor their loved ones ever imagined. You can plan all you want, but in the end, life takes its own course.

The morning after our talk, I took the earliest possible flight to Phoenix -- my third trip to Arizona in four weeks. I arrived at the hospital to visit with my aunt only to find a much different environment from the week before. The continued support of a respirator had only served to intoxicate my aunt's lungs, to keep them from working on their own. Her body, increasingly dependent on external machines to perform basic functions, had quietly handed over control to the medical staff. Gone were the brief windows of communication we'd shared the week before through simple hand squeezes and gentle nods of her head. A week of medical challenges had erected a wall of silence between us.

The next day, after collecting a half-dozen medical opinions from doctors directly caring for my aunt, I made a decision. Sitting alone in her hospital room with a book by Scottish poet Robert Burns – her favorite -- resting on my lap, I again prayed for guidance. I thought back to her instructions, which we'd revisited only a month before, and how she'd like me to manage her care if she became incapacitated. Her condition prevented her from communicating with me any longer, but I could clearly hear her voice. Neither of us ever envisioned the situation we were now in together. The Living Will resting beneath the book of poetry weighed heavily on my heart, its legalese ambiguous at best that particular afternoon.

Throughout that night, I again prayed for help in making the biggest decision many of us will ever face for a loved one. The next day I shared my decision with our family. Although it was painful for us all, their support meant the world to me.

As is many times true, much good resulted from our family's journey. Today, after experiencing my aunt's passing together, we share an unyielding bond forged by God's will and our love for each other. And if I know my aunt, this powerful result would be her will, too. ●

82 Daughter Challenges Dad's Wardrobe Choices

"What fashion is that supposed to be?"

My 12-year-old daughter is merciless when it comes to her opinion of my wardrobe.

"You don't like this look?" I asked, expecting maybe a slight thaw in her demeanor. Instead, she cocked her head and looked down her nose like a hunter sighting its helpless target. I'm dressed in a blue suit with a freshly pressed striped dress shirt. I've left the tie at home.

"Please, maybe you should take me shopping for you sometime," she said. "Then maybe you might have a chance of having some real style."

As a father, I value my daughter's opinion of me — within reason. I've always wanted her to look up to me, think of me as her "knight in shining armor," so to speak. What I didn't realize is somewhere along the line my armor would begin to lose its luster in her eyes.

Recently, I took her with me to pick up a new suit.

"Want to help pick out a tie for me?" I asked.

Laying the black pinstripe suit across the counter, I turned her loose. She walked over to a pair of circular tables with ties fanning across each and began to make suggestions.

How about this?" she said, indicating a bright red tie aggressively contrasting against the white shirt I had chosen.

"I don't know about that one," I said politely, hoping her second pick might be a bit more muted.

"Okay," she said, choosing one with a blend of orange and red. "How about this?"

Thinking about the conservative event I'd be wearing the suit for the next day I felt a chill originating at about my feet. Originally, I'd figured there couldn't be too many ties in the store I wouldn't feel comfortable wearing — and then my self-appointed fashion assistant began making suggestions.

I guess one day we all come to the conclusion we just might not be as cool as we thought. I just needed a 12-year-old to cut to the chase. For the past couple years she's been making remarks about how my wardrobe lacks what she calls "style." Unfortunately for me, her preferences for me run a bit toward a spectrum of bright colors generally reserved for the fresh fruit and vegetable aisles of the grocery store. My mother purchased clothes for my brother and me based on our eye color - mine brown, his blue - and here my daughter is desperately attempting to break me out of my comfort zone. And as a matter of fact, my wife had to practically force me to wear a blue dress shirt years ago. Until then, my shirts were all white, just like I'm sure nature intended them to be.

Today I face an aggressive, strong-willed individual who won't exercise the gentle tact my wife extended to me years ago. No, I can see the day coming when she'll be dressing me — and it should be easy to recognize. I'll be the guy wearing the tie that needs no introduction. Please don't point or laugh. A silent, knowing nod, however, will be greatly appreciated. ●

83 Perspectives Altered by Time

Albert Einstein correctly concluded time is relative. What he didn't think to do was apply his theory to parenting.

"How are the kids doing?" I asked a friend earlier this week. I'd first met her children what seemed just a few years ago -- until I did the math. In truth, nearly a half-dozen years had elapsed since I'd seen her son and daughter.

"He's now as tall as me," she said of her son.

I could still see her son, sitting at his mom's desk, wearing a Cubs baseball cap and a charming smile. As he struggled to sit up straight in her chair and keep his arms horizontal on the surface of her desk, he scribbled with magic markers on a piece of paper taken from her printer. It reminded me of a few days earlier, when I first looked through a recent batch of pictures I'd taken of my own children. Funny how time seems relatively static when you're around someone each day and yet you are surprised at a photo taken moments before.

My son, now 16 years old, projects a strong maturity through his photograph, something I'd missed from across the dinner table at night. Today I can clearly see both of his worlds, one reflecting the innocence of his youth and another marking his evolving independence and strength while entering the adult world. He is, without question, letting go and moving on.

On the other hand, the outside changes in his 12-year-old

sister are far more obvious, as she constantly challenges us with her wardrobe. Her face, too, reveals someone I didn't expect to meet for another few years. I have to fight the urge to accept that her face is one of a high-school teenager in one particular photo. She is projecting the many of the same characteristics her brother does. It is an unsettling feeling, one I'm sure I share with many other parents. Einstein's theory plays out as a simple reminder that the world looks much different when we step back and look at it from a distance. To those outside of our daily world, changes in our children are viewed much differently – like when I think of my friend's son. To me, he will always be drawing at his mother's desk, wearing a Cubs baseball cap and a grin. But to her, with changes occurring right beneath her nose, growth is subtle until one day he reaches a milestone like being as tall as she is.

Our conversation bounces between different subjects, but when my friend and I end our chat, I can't help seeing an image in my mind, one of the little boy who lives in his Cubs cap quickly growing up into a young man while his mother stands beside him, watching. ●

84 Spring Break Is Not Just for Kids Anymore.

"I'm leaving for Spring Break in the morning," my friend announced. "Eleven hours on the road, but well worth it."

He and I, roughly the same age, share memories of MTV and Spring Break as something more than just a few days off from class. These days, he's traveling with his wife and kids and staying at beachside resort. Long gone are the days of sleeping bags, late nights and cramming as many friends as possible into a cheap hotel room.

"You know you're getting older when you've got 'nap plans' and a handful of books to read under an umbrella," he joked.

"I understand," I said, a twinge of jealousy beneath my words.

I have to laugh at the irony. Oh, how a couple of decades have changed us, the Spring Break pioneers. Like my friend, I'd gladly trade the good old days of Spring Break for a long afternoon nap and a good book. If this is getting older, sign me up.

Years ago, Spring Break did not exist as the marketing juggernaut it is today. When I shared that information with my own children, they were shocked. The generation who helped elevate its status from a couple days off from school into an annual rite of passage is beginning to show its age. No longer are we drawn by its endless – and sometimes mindless -- contests and cheap entertainment. No, today we are discovering a brand-new set of activities to meet our Spring Break dreams. Loud music? No thanks. Give me some peace and quiet, an umbrella and a lounge chair near the pool. That I can work with. Food? Keep the pizza. I need something lighter on the calories, hold the trans-fats please. I might be on vacation, but my doctor will eventually find out about any indiscretions with a cheese dog and fries.

Yes, with the original Spring Breakers aging gracefully, it just might be time for the marketers to consider changing their pitch. Imagine, if you will, a Spring Break promoting late-morning tee times, fresh fruit breakfast bars, and free wireless signals on the beach. Yes, we're still going on Spring Break, but our needs are a changing with the times. Today, our Spring Break plans include a heavy dose of quiet time.

My friend, who I'm sure never pictured going on Spring Break with his future children way back when, is learning to adjust to his new-found goals in life. For him, as for many of his generation, Spring Break is evolving into a brand-new event, one in which doing the things we want to do the most many times means doing absolutely nothing. Nada. Zip. Zilch.

So this spring, as you flip though the channels and spot an MTV-like Spring Break celebration, take a moment to remember those of us who so proudly blazed the trail decades ago. We're the ones hanging out by the pool with a bottled water and looking forward to our nap time. ●

85 Dad Gets 'Malled' by Daughter

Shopping with my pre-teen daughter is an exercise in negotiation and a competition of wills.

"What size do you wear?" I asked her last week as I browsed through a stack of colored t-shirts.

"Small," she said.

"What size is the t-shirt we're returning?"

"Small."

"We're here because Mom sent us back to return the last shirt we bought together," I reminded her. "Let's not get me in trouble again."

My daughter and I have been spending more time together in a strange, enclosed ecosystem commonly known as a mall. Shopping, for her, is more about the chase than the capture. My shopping practices -- and those of my son -- involve necessary, almost mercenary, missions. Identify your target, plan your action, capture (purchase) and get out in as little time as possible. For us, any shopping excursion lasting longer than 45 minutes is a failed mission, poorly planned and executed.

So I'll admit I'm pretty much out of my element when it comes to shopping with my daughter. What I'm discovering is a brand-new world of challenges. Sizes suddenly seem open to interpretation. Over the past couple weeks, I've seen t-shirts labeled medium that could barely cover a Chihuahua, let alone my daughter.

Fortunately, my wife is patiently coaching me behind the scenes. After the first returned t-shirt incident, she was willing to share some pointers.

"Did she try on the shirt first?' my wife asked me.

"Well, no," I said. "She told me she wore a small. "

You need to make her try things on first," she said.

I looked for a trap and, when I didn't see an obvious one, agreed that sounded like an easy solution. But then she let it slip.

"That means having her come out of the dressing room and you looking at it."

Ugh. Never occurred to me. Most guys – if you can even get us to try something on our bodies instead of just holding it up to our chests – rarely come out of the dressing room unprompted. I believe it somehow reminds us of shopping with our mothers, thus threatening our masculine independence. (Yes, we're that insecure.)

On that afternoon. I began to piece together my daughter's strategy. For 45 minutes she led me around stores in what seemed to be an aimless exercise. But I now realize she was wearing me down. She'd figured out long ago she just needed to outlast my attention span – and then find a store with a comfortable chair for me to sit down in.

I'll admit I was exhausted after her trek through what seemed like endless stores. I'll also admit I didn't implement any of the preventive actions my wife had suggested. I was, I now realize, played by a cool, calculating opponent who knew my limitations.

What happens to me when she turns 12? ●

86 Body Protests Reliving Youth

Earlier this week Father Time rudely slapped me in the face, forever altering my opinion of my physical self.

This spring I'm back on a softball team. Although the name on my driver's license did not change, somewhere along the line I apparently did. I was ready for sore muscles. I was ready for strains. I was ready for rust. What I wasn't ready for was discovering that my brain now operates what appears to be someone else's body.

Like a lot of us, I grew up with a baseball mitt tucked under my bed. By the time I was 10 I could probably recite the 1927 Yankees lineup more readily than the 50 state capitols. Summers not spent playing in a league were spent gathering in the cul-de-sac for pickup games with a worn tennis ball and paper plates for bases. Baseball was my first true love.

But like in many relationships, we eventually drifted apart. My interests began to turn toward a certain skateboard, and my newly found freedom as a teenager gave me even more opportunities to spend with the object of my affection. Quietly my relationship with baseball faded away. My spikes ended up in the back of the closet and I quit oiling my mitt each spring.

Until: "We're starting a softball team," said a co-worker, "You in?"

I could almost smell the leather of my mitt, even though

I wasn't even sure in what part of the house to begin looking for it. Nostalgia overpowered my middle-aged body, and my answer was out before my brain could engage.

"Sure," I said, "I'll play."

Let me tell you, after one practice and one game I've learned a great deal about myself – and its not necessarily anything I wanted to know. It all started with a ground ball to second. Years of coaches drilling infield fundamentals into my mind, and I was able to unearth the instruction manual buried in my memory banks.

"Stay on your toes, lean forward, keep your hands low and bring up some dirt with the ball," I told myself.

What I didn't expect was for my back to immediately complain. Bending over to tie my shoes, already not the most pleasant experience these days, is nothing compared to scraping up dirt on a full run and twisting to throw across your body. One ground ball, one throw and – twinge – welcome to middle age. No longer does my back wish to bend down past my shoes, nor does my body care to turn, twist and throw across my body at full steam, so it sent me a nasty-gram.

"Hey, you" my back said. "Yeah, you with the grey hair sprouting out all over. Just what in the world do you think you are doing to me? I put up with this when you were a kid, but I can tell you right now I won't be doing it again."

Then my ego stepped in.

"Quit your whining down there," it shot back. "We're not old yet. Heck, we're not ready to throw in the towel. Take it like a man and walk it off."

Finishing my throw to first base I attempted to stand up straight again. My back forcefully stated its case again, sending pinpricks of pain to put a point on it.

Another ground ball in my direction, and it was decision time. My back sent yet another harbinger of pain to come as my feet moved forward to take the hop. My ego countered by filling my head with memories of aromatic dirt and grass stains, a peaceful world where the only thing I needed to do - other than play baseball - was to remember to be home in time to eat.

Remembering there was a drug store on the way home, I drove my glove into the loose dirt. After all, I told myself, I have a powerful little friend named ibuprofen. Welcome, my ego said, to a world of better living though the corner pharmacy. ●

87 Screen Door Syndrome Tests Marriages

"I'd heard a lot of remodeling jobs start with a new screen door."

My friend, his home still in disarray from the comings and goings of multiple contractors, looked down at his drink and takes a deep breath.

"I kid you not," he confided. "First a new screen door, then the door didn't match. Then comes the wall color, carpet. Before you know it, the front room is completely redone. And guess what? Couple of weeks later she brings up how it doesn't match the rest of the house, and before I know it, she's gone completely through the house and onto the back deck."

Some of us at the table couldn't help a few chuckles at his expense.

"Never knew a screen door could cost so me much," he said.

As amusing as I considered his comments to be several years ago, I have found myself in an almost identical situation. And yes, it all started with a new screen door.

"How about this one?" my wife said one day at a local hardware store, indicating a door. "It has a retractable screen so we can open up a breeze in the house."

I thought about my friend's cautionary tale, but outside it was warm and a cool breeze sounded good, so I set aside my doubts and said, "Sure."

And so began in our home a year-long project closely following the script my friend prophesied.

Doing work on a house is nothing new for my wife and me. Painting, carpeting and yanking out old landscaping is all pretty standard when we buy a home. We've learned our strengths and weaknesses and so far have survived unscathed, except for a particular wallpapering event we won't talk about. But this time our screen door led to more — much more.

"I've got an idea," my wife said, holding out a piece of paper.

On her sheet of paper I could see lines and, well, more lines. Envisioning from blueprints was never my forte.

"This is a window I'd like to take out and this here — the two lines — is a doorway," she explained patiently. "If we remove this wall ..."

Alarms were going off inside my head as I thought of my friend and how he'd warned me years ago.

"Now what?" I asked myself. "He didn't say what to do when this happens."

My wife continued. "This'll open up all this area here and ..."

Looking at the walls, then back to the lines drawn on the paper, I was utterly lost and confused. Knowing she'd worked the business side of home building for years before we married, I was admittedly outmatched. To me, lines were lines and I really didn't understand what she was saying. But I also knew drawing up and altering house plans was nothing new for her. I knew this day would come — the day I'd have to hand over my trust and checkbook to my wife — and hope we survived. So far, I can tell you, we are still on speaking terms and sleeping in the same bed even as the dust from sanding the wood floors literally settles on every surface in the house. And so far, to her credit, the project is on time and on budget.

The secret to our surviving this chapter of major disruption in our life is simple: I get up each morning, don't ask too many questions and am careful to not let the screen door slam on me when I leave for the office. ●

88 Hammer Drives Dreams to Reality

The difference between an amateur and a craftsman can be determined by a single blow to the head of a nail.

For the past couple of weekends, I've been fortunate to spend time working with a local chapter of Habitat for Humanity as it built a home in our community.

"Hello," said a smiling young woman. "I'm the homeowner. Thank you for coming today."

Her face is radiant. Her hair pulled back in a ponytail, wearing an oversized t-shirt, she walks back to one of many groups assembling exterior walls on the church parking lot.

I am not a craftsman, but I do own a hammer and I want to help. Standing there, crews laying out skeletons of walls across the asphalt parking lot, I realize I'm not alone in either my of desire to help or my uncertainty of how exactly I can best contribute to the process. I soon learn this qualifies me to join the cause.

"I need a dozen two-by-fours," a man wearing a green cap barks from nearby.

One of the founding principles of Habitat for Humanity is that just about anyone can wield a hammer and drive a nail. The price of a simple hardware-store hammer lowers the cost of participation to a few dollars and a few hours of time on a Saturday morning.

I join another man at the lumber pile, and we begin pulling the boards requested by the man in the green cap.

After I introduce myself, my fellow lumber locator tells

me he and his 10-year-old son are working on the project together. Looking over, I see the young man in a red T-shirt carefully dropping two nails below where each board is marked to be joined together. Following behind him is a volunteer who is driving the nails into the white wood. I notice that it takes an average of three blows for a volunteer to successfully drive a long nail into its seat.

Just off the parking lot I see a growing pile of assembled framing walls being set aside as the piles of lumber steadily dwindle.

The more I visit with others at the site, the more I am convinced there must be only a handful of experienced craftsman working alongside us. Green Hat comes over to demonstrate to a volunteer exactly where he'd like the nails driven for a particular area of the frame. He's gentle, yet firm in his instructions.

"Here, and here," he says, deftly driving the nails into the board.

His hammer blows are purposeful and regular, different from the others I have seen. Just two strikes, one to set, one to drive and seat. He demonstrates with another nail left earlier by the young dropper, repeating the efficient, two-strike process.

Returning the hammer to the volunteer, Green Hat moves on to direct another crew working on an interior wall. We all get back to work with our three-strike drives. It doesn't take too much calculation to see the extra time it takes volunteers to construct a frame with one extra strike per nail. But efficiency is not the key to the process. Instead, it is the end result of the volunteers' time and effort.

As our day winds down, the homeowner again works her way around the groups, thanking them for volunteering to help build her a home. I can see honest, heartfelt emotion in her eyes. Another crew, I'm told, is across town doing the foundation work. Next weekend, the walls this cast of volunteers assembled with the simple combination of a hammer, nails and the desire to help others will be erected. And shortly afterward, behind those walls held together with nails hammered in by volunteer novices and craftsmen alike, a family will begin a new life. ●

89 Martians Don't Wear Makeup

"What is that?" I asked.

I'm driving my daughter to junior high when she pulls a small satchel from her purse and opens a bottle of cream.

She looks at me like I've just seen the moon for the first time.

"My makeup bag," she said.

Knowing she'd just spent the better part of the past hour getting ready for school, I couldn't understand why she needed to bring it along.

Returning the cream to her makeup bag, she then extracts a long, dark pencil – and catches me staring again.

"Eyeliner," she said, as if instructing me.

"Why are you taking it to school?" I asked.

"In case my makeup wears off."

"Why would it wear off? It's not like your face is touching anything. Does it evaporate or something?"

Her eyes roll, and not because of the proximity of the eyeliner to her face.

"Da-ad," she said, stretching out the word for emphasis.

I can't let it go.

"Well," I asked, "where is it going? Its not like it blows away, does it?"

I've never worn makeup and I honestly don't understand. Using the pop-theory of "Men are from Mars, women from Venus,"

I guess I'm a full-blooded Martian.

Apparently I'm in the middle of a very dangerous window for the father of any daughter, the window in which she sheds her little-girl image for something new and different. Call it Venus-like. Call me petrified.

"Dad, you just don't understand," she said, flipping the visor mirror back up into place. "It just needs a touch-up now and then."

Again, I need to understand the physics. How does makeup disappear if it is not touched? Once it is on, where does it go? If someone is touching it, and it's not her, I've got worse problems than I thought.

My daughter is proving I don't really know everything after all. Raising her brother is easy, from my point of view. Outside of a few incidents fueled by testosterone, he's pretty predictable. I've been there, understand it and can deal with it. Life on Mars is easy compared to Venus.

Several years ago, when the airlines first began banning liquids over 3 ounces, my wife revealed why so many women were visibly upset around the terminal.

"You don't want to know how much this little tube of makeup cost," she said.

As I looked down at the small, circular jar in her hand — a jar barely big enough to make a decent peanut butter and jelly sandwich — my wife suggested I sit down before she shared its value in dollars. And I'm glad I did.

Which brings me back to driving my daughter to school and discovering she is now carrying around a bag designated for makeup only. If her trading the innocence of childhood for being a card-carrying member of the Venus club wasn't enough, I had to do the math. Not only am I about to lose my little girl, but I'm also going to have to take a pay cut.

Zipping up her case, my daughter turned and looked at me. Her eyes were beautiful, her lashes full. And for a moment, this Martian father lost his place in time. ●

90 Aging Challenged by Self-Perception

My younger brother is now older than me.

As little sense as that would seem to make, anyone with brothers, sisters, cousins, nieces or nephews surely understands. At some point in life we all stop aging, if only in our minds. And after my brother's birthday this month, he is now chronologically older than my mind will ever accept me as being. There is no way I am as old as my younger brother's Arizona driver's license lists him as being.

I'm just not ready to get old. But somewhere along the line, we begin looking at ourselves in the mirror at little less often. And when we do, we spend less time examining our face for wrinkles. I've begun to believe the entire combination of weakening eyes and a few more wrinkles each year is nature's way of helping me manage the shock.

As time moves along, many of us have a perception of what age we really are in our minds. This age – much younger than our chronological age, of course – is where we feel comfortable. It is the age we relate to the best. I feel it, even today, as I look across the living room and realize my wife and I are living with teenagers.

"Whose teenagers are those?" I asked her the other night.

Across the room, our son and daughter sat with the television on, working on a laptop and texting on a cell phone, respectively. Looking back at my wife, I felt as if we're still essentially the same two people who met during our first semester of college. In my mind we've not changed all that much. Sure, we have more responsibilities – and more people to be responsible for – but we're still the same two people who couldn't get enough of each other decades ago. There are times I feel like we're just playing grown-ups and forever will be sitting at the children's table at family gatherings.

Nature is funny about this. I have a good friend who, in his 90's, is as young and vibrant as anyone I've ever known. He's the epitome of a gentleman and as comfortable in his skin as anyone you'll ever meet. I don't know what age he thinks he is, but I'll tell you it in no way matches his birth certificate. Sitting with him recently, I was taken by the sparkle in his eyes and the power of his warm smile as it grew across his face. Just sharing the room with him made me feel better.

I'm going to a wedding next month where I'll see nieces and nephews arrive driving their own cars. Some will even bring dates, spouses and children. This, no matter how much I try to accept it, does not compute with my internal perception of time. To me, they are still just kids. Always will be.

If indeed age is a state of mind -- a feeling of being comfortable in your own skin regardless of what the calendar dictates -- then I'm okay. I just need to get my body to buy into that concept and get with the program. ●

91 Doing Nothing Means Everything

Sometimes the secret to being a parent is just doing nothing at all.

Last week, while out for a morning walk, I stopped to take a rest on a wooden park bench. Looking across the sidewalk I noticed a man with a little boy sitting close beside him. Dressed in a slightly oversized shirt and shorts, the young boy let his feet dangle over the edge of the bench. The man's left arm was lovingly draped across the boy's shoulders, a pose I recognized as a gesture of security for them both.

"Boat," said the boy, pointing out across the water.

Words tumbled from his mouth as the little boy tried to put his excitement into words. Stumbling over sentences, he maxed out his vocabulary as his dad gave him his undivided attention, looking at his son with fascination and pride. No cell phone rang, no newspaper distracted him just then. In that moment, only two people existed in the entire world, and the boat crossing the water was the most interesting event in history.

As I watched the pair, I was reminded that powerful memories can be made even when nothing in particular is happening around you.

Thinking back to my childhood, I found my best memories included not rushing from ride to ride at an amusement park but just hanging out — free of any agenda in particular — with my mom or dad. I still recall sitting at the kitchen table, my mom drinking her coffee and the two of us just talking about what she'd read in the newspaper earlier in the morning.

I remember how my dad, wrestling with my teenage years, skillfully practiced the art of patience, something I hope to learn as my own children continue to grow. If anything, I believe my parents' consistent, caring hands helped me develop a sense of security and comfort in knowing, regardless of what happened, they were always there for me. Our relationship was built on two simple principles: we were in this for the long haul and we all loved each other without question.

As a parent whose own children are now in their teenage years, I just hope I've somehow managed to provide them with the same feeling of security I took from my childhood. We can give our children things — a good education, a particular pair of jeans, a new CD — but the important things they'll carry with them throughout life are ones we can't buy with a check or credit card.

The little boy began fidgeting in his seat, his anxious energy disturbing the moment his father clearly cherished. The father's left hand, large enough to easily cover his son's shoulder and back, gently settled the boy. But I recognized all too well as a parent that their moment would soon end.

I only hope that small boy will one day draw from and appreciate the moment he and his father shared on the park bench for what it was: the art of doing absolutely nothing -- except being there for each other. ●

92 Breakfast Advice Served Over Easy

A long line of customers dressed in t-shirts and cover-ups winds out the door and along the short bank of windows at the beach-side café.

Inside, two men, separated by several decades, are sharing much more than a cup of coffee at breakfast.

"Can I get you gentleman anything else?"

The waitress, tall and energetic, smiles as she pours refills of coffee.

The older man, decorated with a black beret and two diamond earrings, sips coffee from his cup. Gray hair lightly glints at the sides of his dark hair, in sharp contrast with his dark skin. As the waitress moves to the next table, the younger man leans forward, listening attentively. He is athletic, dressed in an oversized basketball jersey, long shorts and basketball shoes.

The older man is talking but not preaching.

"You can always get more money," he said. "And you can always get a job. But remember, you can't always get what is important to you in life."

The actual relationship between the two is not clear but the respect between them is obvious. One is the teacher, the other his student. A small beachside café is not a traditional classroom, and I can't help being moved by their relationship.

At the table beside me is something too rare in the world today: one person taking the time to guide another without using intimidation as his teaching tool. There are no harsh words, no loud words. The strongest element in the conversation is the passion with which the older man is sharing information with his breakfast partner.

Money is temporary in nature. What the older man shares is what a lifetime of experience has revealed to him – that money is transient. You get money. You spend money. Need more? Odds are you'll find a way to get some, through a bank or through your brother.

As for a job, the world is full of them. Some we like, others we don't want to do for any amount of money. The point is that jobs, like money, are transient in nature. What he wants the young man to understand is that there is so much more to life than what a job and money can provide.

"You can't always get what is important to you in life," is what I find haunting. As my life continues to move along the tracks of time, I've found what is truly important to me in my life silently – and without fanfare – changing in the background. At that young man's age, I'll admit, I valued both money and a job highly. But today I understand my youthful self didn't know what the world had in store for me. Never could I have imagined my life-changing experiences with those around me. Family and friends are, without a doubt, the meat and potatoes of life. No amount of money or job satisfaction could ever have compared to the love and friendship I've learned to value as time goes forward. The blessings of life are divine and cannot be purchased with cash or earned by working for a couple of weeks.

The waitress returns and places the check on our table. The crowd outside dwindles as the lunch hour approaches. The two men, still sharing breakfast, remain in place as I leave the diner, hoping valuable words of experience were not lost in translation between their two generations. ●

93 Retirement Not About Slowing Down

Sometimes, the end of the road is not the end of the road.

I recently found myself once again standing inside a small surf shop along the south Atlantic coastline. There is room for me and about a half-dozen customers at best. On this morning, it is just me, a few racks of tee-shirts and an older man behind the counter. Just outside the door, a makeshift rack displays a half-dozen surfboards for sale.

"Good morning," the man behind the counter said, looking up at me over his reading glasses with a smile.

"Morning," I said, returning the welcome. "Nice shop. Yours?"

His smile broadened. He stood up and walked out from behind the counter to shake my hand.

"John," he said by way of introduction. "Yes. Been here a couple years now."

I see a bumper sticker on the counter advertising his shop. "Aloha, y'all," it reads. John is bearing down on 60 years old and has realized his lifelong dream of owning and operating a surf shop. For him, like many today, retirement is not about slowing down but about growing.

"Nice," I said, giving a nod to his shop. "You make your own boards, too?"

"Yes, next door," John said, his eyes lighting up. "Making a six-foot paddle board right now."

Stepping outside, I see a small hutch next door. Aching with curiosity, I ask if I can check it out.

"Sure," he said with a smile. "Just don't get anything on you."

Moments before, John had told me how he'd retired a few years back and decided to chase the only real dream he'd never pursued – handcrafting custom surfboards and selling them out of his own shop. He'd joked if he was much busier he'd have to hire someone, making it feel too much like a job.

"Heck, now when the waves are up I just put a sign on the door saying I've gone surfing," he said. "I leave a small table of surfboard wax out and everyone pays on the honor system. Never been a problem."

John's waves are a long way from the decades he spent in the airline industry.

"This is just one thing I always wanted to do for me," he said. "I grew up in California and while everyone else was surfing or hanging out at the beach, I was working or going to school. I spent my spare time helping shape boards during the summer but life somehow just got busy. One thing led to another and when I retired from the real world I decided to chase this dream down."

Stepping into the small building next door I gently squeeze next to the paddleboard resting on its back like an upside-down turtle, its fins pointing upward. Dust from the sanding of the fiberglass covers every inch of the building. Wooden templates with hand-written notes lean against the walls. I look down at the long, white board beneath the hanging light and notice a small marking. Looking closer I realize the marks are a hand-scrawled signature of the artist whose hands gently shaped the lines of the graceful fiberglass canvas.

I return to the shop and put a tee-shirt and bumper sticker on the counter. They will remind me that life is not about the destination but the journey. And how for some of us, the journey just might include never letting go of our dreams -- even if it means wearing our surf shorts to work every day. ●

94 Does Memory Loss Lead to Bliss?

If this is what life in my 40s is like, I'm terrified at what could be around the corner. First, my knees began complaining about years of running along the side of the road. Next, my weight began ignoring changes I made to my diet, leaving me to falsely accuse the dry cleaners of tightening my pants. Now – before I even hit my mid-40s – I'm pretty sure I losing my mind.

"You called yesterday?" said the voice on the other end of the telephone.

I instantly recognized the voice, but found myself unable to remember why I'd called him. I began treading water, asking questions totally unrelated to any business conversation I'd surely called him about. We talked about golf and family while I searched the recesses of my mind, and then I confessed.

"Rick, to be honest, I don't have the slightest idea why I called you," I said. "It is completely gone. I don't know what is happening these days. Tell me this gets better."

He asked my age. Fortunately, that was a fact I was able to recall without whipping out my driver's license.

"Look, we're about a decade apart," Rick said. "I can promise you in no uncertain terms it indeed gets better."

"How so?" I asked suspiciously.

"When you're my age you'll not only have forgotten why

you called the day before but even the fact you made the call in the first place," he said. "It's actually quite comforting."

Sounded more like a massive dose of bliss to me.

I don't know about you, but I think this aging thing is scary. When you're looking at it from the point of view of youth, you tend to identify the obvious external indicators: a wrinkle here or there, a paunch pushing at the belt line. What I never anticipated was the battle I would have to fight between my own two ears.

"You know," one of my dearest friends said to me earlier this year, "the hardest thing about growing older is not being able to remember the names that go with all the faces I've met over the years."

My friend, in his ninth decade, has earned the right to forget a few things along the way. Still, he was pained in his confession.

Life is an interesting ride full of unexpected twists and turns. But today, with both my body and mind showing signs of wear and tear. I'm a bit more sensitive to the little episodes that can't easily be addressed with a couple of ibuprofen tablets.

More than two weeks have passed since I experienced my watershed moment – leaving a voice mail to a friend and not being able to recall why I first picked up the phone just 24 hours later. What worries me is what might be coming down the road that I don't know about. Who knows? Next I might find myself forgetting my cell phone number. On second thought, strike that one – I already get it wrong about half the time. ●

95 Cocoon Opens Before Dad's Eyes

Friends warned me this day would one day come.

"Dad, I'm practically a teenager," said my daughter the other night.

"You're twelve," I said. "Sorry, but that's not a teenager."

"It's a pre-teen. And in another six months I'll be thirteen."

Crossing her arms for emphasis, she snapped her head slightly to the side as if to say "in your face." As much as I believed the facts were on my side, something told me even if I won the argument I'd already lost the battle.

"Just you wait," I remember a good friend telling me years ago. She was managing a pair of teenagers at home as my children were just entering school. "Don't laugh. Your day is coming."

Truer words, I now realize, we never spoken.

Why is it boys seem comfortable in their own skins, not in any particular in a hurry to grow up except to get a driver's license? Time moves on and they are pretty much along for the ride. Girls, on the other hand – my daughter a textbook case – seem to be racing Father Time. It starts with earrings, moves on to nails and next thing you know you've lost track of what their natural hair color might be.

I miss my little girl. Looking back though photos on the computer the other night, I saw someone who I felt I've not seen in nearly a decade only to realize the blossoming of this new person occurred inside of two years. With the exception of her eyes, everything was changing – and not just cosmetically.

Comparing the old photo to the person in the other room watching television, I could see so many of the changes that had sneaked by in daily life, their gradual nature masking dramatic changes. Gone was the shy little girl, replaced by someone with a strong sense of self-confidence. Any hint of timidity, a natural childhood trait, has disappeared in this person who will now share her opinions in the blink of an eye.

She is my youngest, so this is a very difficult change for me to accept. She is – and always will be – my little girl.

As I talk with friends who've watched helplessly as their little girls grow up, I know all is not lost. According to my friends, they will always hold memories of when they first saw their little girls – and of when they realized their daughters had become young women. As difficult as it was for them to be on the sidelines, watching their daughters break free from the cocoon of childhood and move into the world of womanhood was another unexpected blessing that came with raising a daughter. Additionally, I'm told, no matter what her driver's license might say or how strongly independent she becomes, a daughter will always share a unique and special bond with her father.

And as the father of a daughter, it is that bond I hold dearest to my heart. ●

96 Even Pigs Understand Character Matters

Regardless of what many in today's society might have us believe, character matters.

From a professional football player standing in a courtroom facing dog fighting charges to an NBA referee directly linked to an illegal gambling investigation, some would like us to believe these are just misunderstandings or proof we are all human. Despite fame, wealth and popularity, paid spokespeople trumpet, people are not role models unless we appoint them as such. It's our fault if we - or our kids - we choose to look up to them.

They should've listened to my mother.

I remember her telling me a story she'd heard as a child, growing up in a small village in Scotland. It's one I've even passed along to my own children.

"One day," she said, "an old man and woman are walking down a village dirt road. Coming around the corner, they notice a large puddle of mud where the town drunk and a large pig are sitting and sunning themselves. The woman turns to her husband and says under her breath, 'You sure can tell someone's character from the company they choose to keep.'"

My mom would always insert an awkward pause at this point in the story.

"And with that," she would finish, "the pig promptly got up and walked out of the mud puddle."

It was a great old story, one I've remembered my entire life.

"Remember," my mom said after each telling of the story, "you've only one good name. "Don't mess it up. If you're in doubt of who to hang around, just ask yourself if you'd like other people to think of you in those terms."

Her words made a big difference to me. It wasn't about being the perfect kid, but about whether I wanted someone else's bad choices to reflect on me. Particularly in high school, an environment in which drugs and dangerous behavior seem to gain traction, her words always resided in the forefront of my mind. Not that I didn't hang around with a wide range of friends, just that I distanced myself from those whose character I didn't want to emulate. We should never let others' opinions supplant our own when we choose our friends, but in the same vein, we need to recognize that calculating the risk of those friends is our responsibility.

Today's headlines, however, clearly show someone didn't get that message. Routinely, we see young professional athletes earning millions of dollars who are unable to grasp the simple fact that while they may be decent guys, their choice of associates could bring them down in a heartbeat.

Life is made up of the choices we make. Some are good, others, not so good -- a concept so simple even a pig can understand it. ●

97 Death Key to Living Full Life

I'm not sure I want to live forever.

Funny how we all carry a natural desire to never die, yet the older we get, the more we see that living forever might not be the most attractive option. I'm learning this lesson from a front-row seat as my dad approaches his eighth decade and his social calendar becomes increasingly filled with the funerals of close friends and family.

Don't get me wrong, this is not a depressing thought, but an appreciation and understanding of our place in the cycle of life. To have lost someone to death means you first must have experienced closeness to another human being, an intimate bonding of person to another. It is truly the most valuable gift we can share in our lifetime.

My dad sent me an e-mail this week about a very close friend who is wrestling with the onset of a serious medical condition.

"His son is going to drive him to Mayo this week," my dad wrote. "He was told not to fly. No doubt a tenuous situation."

As children, we are privy to our parents' pain as they lose friends and family. Our hearts ache because their hearts ache. For a child, death can be a strange, scary enigma – something we fear and don't understand. I remember one night waking up in my bed crying, absolutely terrified because I was going to die one day. My mother came and comforted me until I cried myself out. She then sat on alongside me on my bed and explained how life works, how no one gets to live forever here on earth.

"Someday we'll all be together again in heaven," she said. "Just don't you worry."

With her words, the fear slowly began to leave me. But I'll always remember my strange and powerful realization that my parents, my friends and I would all one day be gone.

As we get older, we begin to better understand our place in the world and how love comes with both happiness and sorrow. At the recent funeral of a very dear friend who'd live a long and full life, an elderly man welcomed me as I approached the door to the church.

"You know you've lived a long time when you outlive most of your friends and family," he mused.

He led me into the church, his slow, careful steps testifying to his generous age. As I entered the sanctuary, his words close to my thoughts, I scanned the pews for those who share my friend's generation. Their number, not surprisingly, was modest.

I love my family and friends with all my heart. But as I learned on the side of my bed as a child, our life is a balance of the amount of love and friendship we can create and a deadline on a calendar we cannot read. ●

98 Advice Rings True for Parents

"You hear people say your kids grow up fast," he said to me. "But you don't believe it until it happens right under your nose."

My friend, like many of us, is painfully aware how wise words from experienced parents ring true when put to the test of time.

With another school season off and running, many of us find ourselves in new territory as our children move up the maturity ladder. Earlier this week another friend, sitting across from me in a business meeting, shared with me the sorrow of leaving his youngest child at college the week before.

"My daughter was crying as we left," he said. "But it didn't really hit me until my wife and I pulled into the driveway at home. For the first time, both her car and her older brother's car were gone. It was the loneliest night of our life."

He and his family are as close as any I've ever seen, so I couldn't help but feel a twinge of his pain. Another friend's daughters are speeding through elementary and moving on to middle school, said he has trouble keeping up with how quickly the years are flying by.

Sometimes its hard to remember what grade they are in," he confessed.

Closer to home, I'm living with a monumental change

in my morning routine with our son carrying a driver's license around in his jeans pocket. Since his earliest days in elementary school, he and I have driven to school together. It's been like capturing an extra bit of one-on-one time together to talk about whatever is on his mind. Over the years, this accumulation of time yielded us a generous amount of time to bond and grow together. The conversations – just between the two of us – are among the most special moments of my life, something I will always hold close to my heart. With the start of each new grade level I'd meet a new and different carpool partner as his mind and interests grew in more directions than I could ever imagine.

This year, however, is slightly uncomfortable. No longer is my tag-team partner sitting in the passenger seat as we pull out of the driveway. Now my days include the sound of the garage door opening and catching a passing glance of the rear of a backpack going out the door. Driving himself to school is a milestone he couldn't get to soon enough, as far as he is concerned. But for me, his new chapter is a bittersweet experience. Some mornings, after my son is already gone and my wife and daughter have left for school, the house plays a loud, strange soundtrack of silence.

Fortunately for me, the silence is temporary. I can still take comfort in knowing at night the sounds of life will have returned to occupy their rightful place. But if I've learned anything in the past decade, it is to respect the advice of those who've walked this path before me. ●

99 Dad Needs a Hug

"What are you doing?" I asked my daughter as I was driving her to school earlier this week.

You'd think I would know better by now.

"Putting on makeup," she promptly replied

"In the car?"

"Yes," she said, "Get used to it."

Her sly smile holds a double meaning. Being the father of a young teenage girl can be pretty trying at times.

"Why didn't you put it on at home?" I asked.

"Because I can do it in the car on the way to school," she said. "It saves me time."

She switches from a strange little triangle sponge to something that looks like a pencil with a fuzzy little worm attached to the end, her steady hand adjusting to my shifting the gears of the car.

The past couple of months have been challenging for me as a dad. My little girl now primarily resides in my heart and in the picture frames scattered throughout our home. No longer is holding hands in public acceptable, nor is my arm around her welcome. I know she loves me, but I'm now having to learn to interpret the special code she's developed.

"I love you" has been replaced by the subtle blowing of a kiss across the room as she leaves with friends. Hugs now take place exclusively at home and are generally followed by a couple quick pats on the back -- the signal for "hug's over." To my sorrow, gone are the days when her hugs were for as long as she could get me to let her sit in my lap. Now if find myself thinking, "If only I'd held on a little longer." These days, I ache for the hugs where she'd try to squeeze the breath out of me or attempt to lift my feet up off the ground.

The growing up of all children occurs over a natural passage of time, but when it comes to your youngest child, emotions let you know reality has begun to sink in. I can almost hear the grains of sand accelerating though the proverbial hourglass, and there is nothing I can do to slow them. Her older brother has his sights set on going away to college already, and she is right behind him. Time with our children at home is down to a few short years for my wife and me.

As my daughter and I pulled up to the school, she quickly closed up her makeup case, pushing it deeply into her purse.

"Bye," I said. "Have a good day."

I know she said something but her words were muffled against the outside noise.

Grabbing her purse and book bag, she quickly jumped out of the car and raced off towards the school. For a moment I found myself watching her walk away.

"How can my little girl be a young woman already?" I wondered.

Putting the car back in gear I pulled away from the school, deep in my memories. Gone is the little girl who once begged me to walk her through the front door and all the way to her classroom. Gone, too, is the girl who timidly hesitated at the doorway, turned and gave me a hug before joining her classmates. What is not gone is my memory of a special season in my life with my daughter, one that I'd give anything to relive just one more time. ●

100 Love Secret Ingredient in Mortar of Life

During a drive along a quiet two-lane highway earlier this week, lyrics on a CD playing in my car unexpectedly broke through to me on a very personal level.

"I don't know where I end and you begin," sang the artist.

Out of nowhere, an otherwise innocuous moment sometimes penetrates your exterior and grabs hold of the most sensitive part of your heart. It's funny, but at that moment I knew the simple, familiar song lyric exactly describes my feelings for my wife and children.

In my teens and early 20s, life was all about me. I had responsibilities then, but they were always negotiable. My day-to-day decisions impacted me and no one else. The results — good or bad— were mine and mine alone to deal with at the end of the day. In college, when I made the decision to invite the beautiful girl sitting behind me in history class out to lunch, everything changed.

The transformation didn't happen overnight. Best I can figure, my life simply became increasingly entwined with that of my future wife – the beautiful girl from my history class – until we became emotionally inseparable. Falling in love, I believe it is commonly called.

It's been nearly 25 years since we started down this road,

and I wouldn't turn back for anything. "For better or worse" was part of our wedding vows, and I remember wondering how those words could ever apply to us. God in his grace makes sure we fully understand those words over the course of a lifetime.

I believe that kind of love and commitment is the mortar between the bricks used in building the foundation of a life to-gether. Love means trusting another person enough to hand over the throttle to your heart to him or her. Your pain will never be so deep, and your highs will reach a level you could never imagine. Once you truly love someone, you'll never again be the same person again.

This is why those song lyrics reached down so deeply into my subconscious, stirring my deepest feelings. I honestly don't know where I stop and my wife begins.

Long ago, I never imagined such deep emotions existed. And if I had, the whole idea would have scared the daylights out of me. But today I can't imagine a day, an hour or a moment in which I could ever wish to change what we've become together. She is me and I am her.

Earlier this year, I read an obituary of a good man who passed away soon after losing his wife. The college student I once was might have viewed this as a strange coincidence, may-be even tried to figure the odds of such a thing happening. But the man I am today, the husband and father who understands the creation of the mortar that cements together the bricks of life, knows there is something far more powerful at play.

But only if you've the courage to fully experience love. ●

Leonard Woolsey is married to his college sweetheart. They and their two children live in Georgia.

This is Leonard Woolsey's second published collection from his award-winning, family-based column *In Plain View*.

You can reach Leonard Woolsey at inplainview@charter.net

To purchase additional copies of this book, please visit your local bookstore or contact Broken Moon Media directly at brokenmoonmedia.com